Ghosts of Hollywood II: Talking to Spirits

Marla Brooks

Schiffer
Publishing Ltd

4880 Lower Valley Road, Atglen, Pennsylvania 19310

Cover image
© Thomas
Brostrom.
Image from
BigStockPhoto.
com.
Ouija® is a
registered
trademark
of Parker
Brother's
Games.

Copyright © 2008
by Marla Brooks
Library of Congress
Control Number:
2008928008w

"Schiffer," "Schiffer Publishing Ltd. & Design," and the
"Design of pen and ink well" are registered trademarks of
Schiffer Publishing Ltd.

Schiffer Books are available
at special discounts for bulk
purchases for sales promotions or
premiums. Special editions, including
personalized covers, corporate imprints,
and excerpts can be created in large
quantities for special needs. For more
information contact the publisher:

Published by Schiffer Publishing Ltd.
4880 Lower Valley Road
Atglen, PA 19310
Phone: (610) 593-1777;
Fax: (610) 593-2002
E-mail: Info@schifferbooks.com

Please visit our web site catalog at
www.schifferbooks.com
We are always looking for people to write books
on new and related subjects. If you have an idea
for a book, please contact us at the above address.

This book may be purchased from the
publisher. Include $5.00 for shipping. Please
try your bookstore first. You may write for a
free catalog.

In Europe, Schiffer books are distributed
by: Bushwood Books
6 Marksbury Ave., Kew Gardens
Surrey TW9 4JF, England
Phone: 44 (0)208 392-8585
Fax: 44 (0)208 392-9876
E-mail:
Info@bushwoodbooks.co.uk

Website:
www.bushwoodbooks.co.uk
Free postage in the UK.
Europe: air mail at
cost. Try your
bookstore first.

Designed by Stephanie Daugherty
Type set in A Charming Font Expanded/Hollyweird/NewBskvll BT
ISBN: 978-0-7643-2997-5
Printed in China

Dedication

To Lena, Henry, Rusty, Bill, Gil, Grace and Green Eagle, who are never very far away.

Acknowledgements

It's not always easy to find petople who are willing to give it their all to get the job done, but I've been quite fortunate to have met and worked with some of the best. My undying thanks goes to Victoria Gross, Barry Conrad, and Scott Michaels who are always up for a new investigation despite their busy schedules and to Dinah Roseberry at Schiffer Books who makes it all so easy.

A special nod goes to David Wells, who in spite of being "hectic to a stupid degree," managed to once again make time to write a wonderfully informative foreword to the book and share some of his behind the scenes experiences at The Winchester Mystery House.

And finally, this book could not have been completed without the generosity of Kenny Kingston, Hanz Holzer, Alexandra Holzer Gargiulo, Michael J. Kouri, Richard Senate, and Robert Wlodarski.

Thank you one and all.

Author's Note

For lack of a better term, this is a book a of séances conducted not only by me and my "team" but also those from some of the most well-respected paranormal investigators and psychics of our time.

It should be noted that a séance can be conducted in a variety of ways with any number of people. Some, like the sitting we conducted at Boardner's Bar are formal gatherings with several people in attendance. Others documented in this book were comprised of just two people, like the ones where psychic Victoria Gross and I went out by ourselves and investigated a few reported hotspots whose owners would probably have frowned upon a group of people gathering together to talk to their resident ghosts and scaring their patrons away.

Hollywood séances are no different than séances held in Denver or Des Moines, except for the fact that some of the spirits that come through are quite famous, and as you will see in the following pages, some of those famous Hollywood entities did have good (and sometimes controversial) reasons to do so.

In these pages, you will find that without a doubt, we are *Talking to Spirits*!

Foreword

A séance is a meeting place, an opportunity to communicate formally, with rules if you like; it's a ritual, and like all rituals, it's doing things a certain way that sends a signal to our own subconscious that this is what we are about to do and everything should go into automatic—the routine begets energy that's more powerful the more you repeat it.

If you can sit with the same people all the time, this builds trust and enables a few people to join their energies making ten-fold the impact into the astral worlds; and always have the same opening ritual, again, it says *here I am ready to work* and *I am working with respect and of course protection*. Protection can be as simple as the Lord's Prayer or as complicated as you want to make it—just do it with respect and, above all, *belief* in what you are doing. For an added layer of personal protection invoke your doorkeeper guide, the protector of your crown and don't worry if you don't know who he or she is—just say you want their protection; they know who they are and that's what matters!

Have a trained medium present, they will control who communicates and above all why; it's not like dialing a telephone—it's more like sending up a light to attract anyone who sees it, so control is important, no, crucial. The joining of hands isn't necessary; it's a way of showing that nobody is up to mischief and it has no real impact on the energy.

That happens through your chakras, mainly the heart and solar plexus, which is why some people either feel chest pain or sick during a séance. If you do feel this way wiggle your fingers and feet, remind yourself of your earthly existence and take a deep breath or two whilst you're at it.

If you feel anything, say so. Chances are someone else will be feeling the same; if you get an impression of a name, place, date—anything at all—speak up and if you get physical phenomena, ask them to repeat it at least once. That way you know it's not an old house creaking or a dog whining outside the window.

If you do have anyone famous come through, ask for little known details, date of birth, death, and what they achieved is all well and good, but what was their favourite breakfast, who was their best friend, or what was their first pet? That done, don't forget to ask for real words of wisdom; have they really made all that effort to chat about Snowy the cat? Of course not, they want to let you know about the existence of life after death and what is it like—it's not easy to think of things to ask when you're in that position, so simply say, *Is there anything you want to tell us*; in fact, that goes for whoever comes through, famous or not.

Above all relax, if you're uptight the energy will be spiky; it will have peaks and troughs, and talking of troughs, if you're all exhausted, very little is likely to take place, so make sure you go into your séance as fresh as you can.

Finally remember to have a closing ritual, shut things down with as much enthusiasm as you opened up, and always say thank you—that's just manners!

—David Wells

Contents

Introduction

"We have no reliable guarantee that the afterlife will be any less exasperating than this one, have we?"

—Noel Coward

eople have been trying to contact the dead by means of a séance since the third century but it wasn't until the mid 1800s, when the Spiritualist movement began here in the United States, that these sessions became quite popular.

At first, American and European scientists dismissed spiritualism as an entertaining fad and many critics labeled séances as a scam, possibly because the nineteenth-century séances tended to be very theatrical. They usually took place in darkened parlor rooms with the participants sitting around a table that was loaded down with props. Once the lights were dimmed or completely extinguished, the medium asked the participants to close their eyes and join hands while she went into a trance to call the spirits to her. The reason for the darkness was that Spiritualists believed that spirit forms were more easily seen in the dark, but debunkers and skeptics offered another reason for this practice. They said that darkened conditions would easily hide the deception of fraud.

Another necessary ingredient for a successful séance was appropriate music. Most sittings opened with hymns and prayers, and very often the spirits would chime in with ghostly music and melodies coming though instruments like trumpets, horns, and tambourines. Once the séance began, the table would invariably began to move, ectoplasm might form, cold winds would blow across the table, and if the participants were really lucky, someone's great uncle Zeke would magically appear for a split second from behind a nearby set of drapes.

For those who took spirit communications more seriously, it quickly became apparent that they actually were communicating with the other side because many of the messages received from spirit were found to be quite accurate. In addition to the messages, other phenomenon was being witnessed and verified by many of the most credible individuals in American and European society.

Following the loss of so many lives during World War I and the flu epidemic that followed, the desire to contact the dead reached a fever pitch. Scientists then began taking an interest in the phenomenon, as did notable individuals of the time—such as Sir Arthur Conan Doyle, Abraham Lincoln, and Britain's Queen Victoria, who often took part in table-tilting circles.

In the early twentieth century, it was famed magician Harry Houdini who brought the subject of séances to the forefront. During the 1920s, Houdini was well known for his debunking of fraudulent Spiritualist mediums. He did not start out attacking fake mediums because he did not believe in the supernatural. In fact, he had gone to many in an attempt to try and contact his beloved mother, but in the process, he found that many of the mediums he met were frauds and this was when he turned to exposing them, while at the same time, still searching for the truth.

Prior to his death in 1926, Houdini made a vow stating that if it were possible to contact the living from the other side, he would do so. He and a number of his close friends promised that whichever of them died first, he should make every attempt to contact the others by way of a secret code. Shortly after Houdini's death, the famous "Houdini Séances" took place every year on the anniversary of the his passing, but over the next ten years, Houdini's spirit remained silent.

On October 31, 1936, Houdini's widow, Bess, held the "Final Houdini Séance" on the rooftop of the roof of The Knickerbocker Hotel in Hollywood. Coverage was provided by radio and the proceedings were broadcast all over the world.

"Houdini! Are you here? Are you here, Houdini? Please manifest yourself in any way possible. We have waited, Houdini, oh so long! Never have you been able to present the evidence you promised. And now, this, the night of nights. The world is listening, Harry.

Levitate the table! Move it! Lift the table! Move it or rap it! Spell out a code, Harry, please! Ring a bell! Let its tinkle be heard around the world!"

The participants attempted to contact the elusive magician for over an hour before finally giving up. The mournful voice of Bess Houdini then echoed through radio receivers around the world.

"Houdini did not come through. My last hope is gone. I do not believe that Houdini can come back to me—or to anyone. The Houdini shrine has burned for ten years. I now, reverently, turn out the light. It is finished."

While Houdini's ghost did not come back that night, a freak storm occurred right after the memorial candle had been extinguished. Strangely enough, the thunder, lighting, and rain it produced occurred only above the Knickerbocker Hotel where the séance participants had been sitting. The rest of Hollywood remained dry. This led some members of the press to speculate that this was Harry Houdini's way of signaling his presence from beyond the grave.

Hollywood joined the séance bandwagon shortly thereafter and it was suddenly chic to believe in the afterlife.

Actress Mae West was very psychic and called upon the "Forces," as she referred to them, every day of her life. She claimed that they assisted her in writing her plays and films, in other business matters, and in her everyday life. Mae regularly hosted séances in her old home in the Ravenswood Apartments on Rossmore Avenue in Hollywood.

The late actress Greta Garbo's involvement with the occult was a lifelong interest that she held dear to her heart. She once said,

"I didn't have anyone to whom I could talk freely, so I went to occultists, devil worshippers, mind readers, and those who occupied themselves with the summoning of spirits. Because I believed in life after death, I kept trying to talk to my father and Moje. During my dreams I heard their voices—terrible, angry voices..."

While interest in the paranormal never died down completely over the years, it reached new heights in the early 1960s when parapsychologist Hans Holzer, the original *Ghost Hunter*, began writing a series of best selling books on the subject of ghosts and the afterlife. Along with mediums Sybil Leek and Ethel Johnson-Meyers, Holzer drew millions of readers into the supernatural realm as he conducted séances in prominent haunted locations all over the world.

With the success of Dr. Holzer's books came a renewed interest in contacting the dead, but this time around, it was the spirits of famous people that were being summoned back from beyond the veil. New York psychic Ronaldi Mendius claims to have contacted JFK at a famous séance at American philanthropist and socialite Brooke Astor's townhouse in October of 1965 where details about Kennedy's assassination were supposedly revealed.

Psychic to the Stars Kenny Kingston, who had always been known for contacting the spirits of the rich and famous, appeared on more television shows than any other psychic, guesting repeatedly on major talk shows around the world. He was the host of two television series, *Kenny Kingston: A Psychic Experience* and *The Kenny Kingston Show*. The mail response was tremendous and he often received in excess of 10,000 letters each week. He was also a regular on *The Merv Griffin Show* and *The Mike Douglas Show* for many years.

Interest in the paranormal was at an all time high and séances to contact the dearly departed were featured prominently in books, movies, and on television. Hollywood played its part in 1990 with the production of *Ghost* starring Patrick Swayze, Demi Moore, and Whoopi Goldberg. The tagline for the film, "A love that will last forever" brought hope to people who had suffered the loss of a love that their dear ones were still around...in spirit. Those *in the know* claim that this film is the closest thing to actual fact that Hollywood has ever produced.

The late writer-director Anthony Minghella followed suit the following year with the British film, *Truly Madly Deeply*, starring Alan Rickman and Juliette Stevenson. Reviewers referred to it as "The Thinking Person's" *Ghost*, and said that the film addressed the reality of the situation and that anyone who has lost a love to an untimely death would surely relate to this film.

In the New Millennium, interest in the paranormal continues to grow, partly due to the myriad of television shows dealing with the subject. This recent surge all began in 2000 when the SciFi Channel created a sensation by producing a nightly thirty-minute show with New York medium John Edward. Then, medium James van Praagh brought the paranormal to network television with *Beyond* in September 2002. Shows such as *Ghost Whisperer* and *Medium* call tremendous media attention to the afterlife and with the great success of reality shows came The Travel Channel's *Most Haunted* and the Biography Channel's *Dead Famous: Ghostly Encounters*, both of which have helped fan the psychic flames by regularly conducting on-air séances.

In true Hollywood style, Pay-Per-View television wasn't to be left out and in 2003 a historic (and lucrative) event unfolded as famed psychics from around the world conducted a séance to contact the late Princess Diana. That was followed in 2006 by another televised Pay-Per-View séance, this time to contact the late John Lennon. *The Spirit of John Lennon* and *The Spirit of Diana* specials became international television events that captivated viewers because, after all, celebrity watching and ghost hunting seem to be two of our nation's favorite pastimes.

The immense popularity of Hollywood séances does have its drawbacks, though, because just like back in the days of old, there are frauds out there who try and cash in on the popularity of the paranormal, whether it be for their own personal gain, or just to draw in ratings. This was brought to my attention not long ago while watching an episode of *Criss Angel Mindfreak*. Angel took a group of celebrities to the very haunted Amargosa Hotel in California's Death Valley Junction and scared the living daylights out of them. While his attempt to contact the spirit of a little girl who was murdered in room 34 looked authentic and his celebrity guests were close to wetting themselves throughout the program, this was just another of Angel's famous illusions and a good attempt to jump on the paranormal bandwagon. Towards the end of the broadcast, a consultant to the show named Banachek commented, "As a magician, you have to understand human nature and be able to take it and weave it to what you want it to do, to the point where you can take people on a psychological terror ride, and that's exactly what Criss did." At the very end of the show Angel asks viewers, "Do you believe in ghosts? I don't."

So there you have it. Sometimes it's hard to know what or who to believe, so my best advice in these matters is, "Trust your gut."

The reason I decided to write a book on Hollywood séances is primarily because, while we were out on previous investigations for my first book, *Ghosts of Hollywood: The Show Still Goes On*, although we did make contact with quite a few spirits, it was just a nodding acquaintance and, for various reasons, we were never able to sit down for a séance and really get to hear their stories. In many cases, these investigations sometimes felt incomplete. After all, these spirits were once alive, and like all of us who still are, they have stories to tell and I think it's important to hear them out, because as anxious as we are to speak with our loved ones on the Other Side (whether it's to make sure they are in "good spirits" or to try and find out where miserly Aunt Tillie stashed those stocks and bonds), they are just as anxious to come through to us—but perhaps for slightly different reasons. You see, they already know how we are, and while some do drop in just to say hello, others have unfinished business or important messages to pass on.

That statement really proved itself true when we recently ventured back to Boardner's Bar in Hollywood to conduct a séance there. The spirit of Hollywood actor Albert Dekker came through loud and clear and asked for our help in clarifying the unsolved mystery surrounding his death.

As with ghost hunting in general, I must offer a warning to those who think contacting spirits is merely a parlor game. Whatever you've heard in the past, please understand that spirits CAN hurt you, and going into an investigation or a séance unprepared can produce some pretty horrific results. It's not uncommon for a spirit to attach themselves to someone and perhaps follow them home only to wreak havoc in their lives for days to come. Please take as many precautions as possible to protect yourself and to insure that your séance experience is a safe one.

The Haunted Bank Vault

I do not fear death. I had been dead for billions and billions of years before I was born and had not suffered the slightest inconvenience from it."

—Mark Twain

At the corner of Hollywood and Highland, just across the street from the world famous Kodak Theater, stands one of our city's oldest and most imposing buildings.

Built by architects Meyer and Holler in 1927 for the sum of $750,000, the office building has had many incarnations over the years. It was called the Pacific-Southwest Trust and Savings, Hollywood First National Bank, and was more recently referred to as the Bank of America building. This historic site, a combination of Gothic and Art Deco architecture, was created by the same architects who designed the world famous Grauman's Chinese Theater just a few doors down. It was the tallest building in the city until 1932 when the Los Angeles City Hall was erected a few miles away in downtown Los Angeles. The building sits among quite a few other historic Hollywood landmarks including the Equitable Building, Taft Building, Guaranty Building, and the Hollywood Professional Building. Most of these edifices housed the financial institutions created to meet the needs of the film industry on the West Coast.

The towering spire, buttresses, and motif of "the Explorers" suggest the sense of fantasy present in Hollywood in that era. The beehive above the entrance

signifies the hope that it would be a "beehive of activity." However, the 1929 stock market crash dashed those hopes and the bank closed.

During the 1950s, the building was often seen on television as one of *Superman's* Gotham City jumping-off points in the series of the same name, and in recent years, a replica of the building can also be found on the Hollywood Boulevard street at the Walt Disney Studio Park in Florida.

I came to find out about the building's haunted reputation when we were out investigating the Hollywood Wax Museum several months ago. Hollywood historian Scott Michaels and I had arrived a little bit early for the investigation and met up with Marc Agena, the museum's operation's manager, in the parking lot behind the museum. While we were waiting for psychic Victoria Gross and paranormal investigator Barry Conrad to arrive, Marc asked us if we'd like to go around the corner and check out his office, which is located in the basement of the bank building.

It was his feeling that the place was quite haunted because he would often hear footsteps, doors slamming, and disembodied voices when he was working down there alone. He also mentioned that something must be wrong with the entire building, because the occupancy rate was so low.

"Right now there are only two tenants in the entire thirteen-story building," he told us, "and that's odd because this is prime Hollywood property. People move in, but they don't stay very long."

As Marc unlocked the front door to let us in, the unlit lobby looked rather scary, as did the old elevator we were about to board. Because of the lobby's décor, there was a definite 'Old Hollywood' feeling in the air, but it wasn't one of those pleasant, welcoming sensations that one might expect from an old, well-used relic. In fact, the whole lobby felt rather "dead."

When we stepped off the elevator and into the cavernous basement, it didn't take a medium to tell us that something down there was not quite right. The air was heavy and the atmosphere foreboding. The building's thick concrete walls completely obliterated the sounds of Hollywood Boulevard up above, and the whole area had a rather morgue-like feel to it.

When we got off the elevator, Marc walked us around the corner and lead us to the main vault. Its huge door was open and I was surprised at how massive the interior was. Now completely empty, it was easy to imagine the space lined with money, important documents and whatever else one keeps in a spectacularly large vault. I had read that many early Hollywood stars banked at Hollywood First National and could just imagine them stopping off to either deposit or withdraw some of their hard-earned savings, or perhaps to stash their jewels or important papers.

With cameras at the ready, we began snapping photos and the results were spectacular. We captured more orbs in five minutes than we'd ever gotten on any of our other investigations put together.

Knowing that Victoria and Barry were probably wondering where Scott and I had wandered off to, we reluctantly left the bank with a promise to come back and conduct a proper séance in the haunted basement. Although we weren't sure whose spirits we might encounter, we were certain that the séance would be exciting.

A few weeks later, the séance was arranged and we met Marc out in front of the building early one Sunday evening. My friend, Virginia Fegley, and her husband, Steve, also joined us for the investigation. Hollywood

Ginny Fegley, Marc Agena, and Barry Conrad.

Boulevard was packed with noisy crowds and walking into the empty building with its deafening silence was an extreme contrast.

We crammed into the small elevator and, for one scary moment when we got down to the basement, the elevator doors didn't seem to want to open and let us out. With my vivid writer's imagination, I silently wondered whether or not that incident was an omen of things to come and was quickly fishing around my purse for my cell phone to see if there was a signal so we could call for help. But the doors did finally open on their own and I quickly dismissed any negative thoughts.

The cavernous basement has long corridors running off in all directions and because this was Victoria's first time there, it was decided that before we sat down for the séance, it might be a good idea to have a walk around and find out which areas held the most spirit activity.

While Barry was setting up his camera to interview Marc about his scary experiences, Victoria, Steve, Ginny, and I ventured out to see who or what we might encounter.

Feeling like rats in a maze, we followed one dark corridor until we came across two smaller bank vaults where Victoria immediately began sensing activity. She told us,

"There's definitely a strong male presence in this area and there's a lot of violence attached to him. The man has black hair and he's white…no, he's telling me he's Hispanic, and he's yelling at me. I think that's because of the hostility surrounding him down here. I think he was shot.

"This happened sometime during the 1930s, and even though he is aware that he has died, he's kind of stuck in limbo and I can't really talk to him. He's one of those spirits that can't be touched because the energy around him is just really violent. It's just swirling and I felt swirling energy around us when we first walked into this area.

"I'm getting the name Robert, and what happened in this area definitely contributed to his death because I see him going up the stairs, beaten up, and there's something going on with the left side of his face. I feel like he was dragged upstairs and while other people may have found him and attended to him, he ultimately died from his injuries.

"I think he was like a security guard because I see him in that type of attire, but this wasn't like a robbery gone bad, it was an inside job.

"What went on down here back in those days?" she asked. "There's just something not legitimate about this bank. I just want to say that things were not as they seemed to be. I'd say there was money laundering going on down here. The upstairs bank was run in a proper manner, but down here there was a lot of shifty things going on and there are a lot of strange characters connected with it."

Because she was not able to help Robert cross over, we left the area and continued on into another room off the corridor where Victoria encountered the spirit of a woman. Her suspicion of 'something not being right' about the area continued as well.

"The female presence is again from the late 1920s to early 30s, and there's also a shape crouching down in that corner over there."

It's interesting to note that before Victoria and I walked into that room, Ginny had tried walk in by herself, but according to her,

A room full of orbs.

"Something stopped me from going in, and it wasn't just because it was dark in there. It felt really cold in the doorway and it was like someone was trying to keep me out."

As with Robert, the female presence was not very communicative, so we decided to return to the main room and rejoin the rest of the group. When we got back, Barry said that he was feeling a bit woozy. "I feel pressure on the back of my skull, some lightheadedness and dizziness."

"That's the same thing Scott Michaels said when he came down here when you guys were here to investigate the Wax Museum," said Marc.

It was then decided that we should all move into the main vault because Victoria was picking up quite a bit of energy in there and suggested that, because it was so active, we should set up for the séance there.

I was a little uneasy about that idea because I kept getting the feeling that once we were all settled down inside the vault, some mischievous entity would shut the massive door on us and we would be trapped. That thought was more the product of an overactive imagination than anything paranormal, but as soon as we began snapping pictures in there, we were again up to our ears in orbs.

"There's a lot of motion going through here," said Victoria, "and that's why I think we're picking up all those orbs with the cameras. This whole area is like a runway with so many people walking back and forth. And again, it doesn't feel like usual bank goings on; it's more like the feeling of illegal activity, like a speakeasy or Mafia sort of feel."

The Vault.

There was a small room down at the far end of the vault with a metal gate and we all thought that might have been the area where the safety deposit boxes were kept. While we didn't pick up anything unusual about the room right then, it did come into play later on during the séance.

"There is so much male energy down here and so many entities in this place," said Victoria, who then suggested that we do a little more exploring to see what else we might pick up before the séance.

As we entered the area of the basement that seemed to be the hub of the building with electrical boxes, generators, and the like, a light seemed to turn on all by itself, and the farther down the corridor we walked, more lights turned on to light the way. We decided that these lights were sensor controlled and began looking for the sensors. For the most part, they were easy to spot, but when we retraced our steps, we found it odd that while the first sensor was just inside the doorway, the light had come on even before we were anywhere near it.

We continued down the long corridor which made quite a few twists and turns past all sorts of tiny little rooms along the way. We finally ended up in a room that looked like a "control room"—for lack of a better word—and began snapping photos of the area. Victoria picked up the spirit of an African-American man who she described as a "service man," not in the Armed Forces sense, but one who had worked in the building.

"He goes back to the 1930s or 40s, and I'm suddenly feeling a sharp pain in my jaw. It feels like I just got hit. I don't think this man died here, but it feels like he got into

Down in the basement.

a brawl with someone down here. I think he's still here because it was a place that this man worked for many years and maybe he comes back to try and settle the score."

At that point, it was decided that we would head back to the vault and set up for the séance, and someone mentioned that after walking around and around the basement so much, it would feel good to finally sit down. It really did feel like we'd been walking for miles.

While Barry and Steve scrounged around for a table and chairs that we could set up inside he vault, Victoria, Ginny and I stopped by Marc's office which is near the elevator bank, and Marc told Victoria about a scary event that happened to him not long ago.

"I was in my office one evening, the only one down here, and I was working with the door closed. Suddenly, I heard some walking towards the door from out in the hall, and then the footsteps stopped. I really thought someone was going to knock and so I waited, but after a while, when I didn't hear anything more, I walked up to the door and just listened. I was still waiting for a knock because I didn't hear anybody walking away, so I finally said, 'Yes?' and when nobody answered, I finally opened the door and nobody was there. It was really weird to hear those footsteps approach the door and then wait for a knock that never came."

Marc told us that his octagon-shaped office had at one time been used as a conference room for the bank. Perhaps the footsteps he heard belonged to a long-ago employee who was (quite) late for a meeting.

Marc Agena in his haunted office.

The Séance

After checking Marc's office, which, according to the pictures we took was an "orb free" zone, we returned to the vault and assembled for the séance. Candles were lit and lights were turned off. While we wouldn't have normally started off by using the Ouija board, Steve had brought along a board that had once belonged to his grandmother, Meta, who he describes as a "natural witch."

"She would always collect herbs and flowers, spider webs, moth wings, and all kinds of stuff, and keep them in little apothecary bottles, and then grind them up with a mortar and pestle when she needed them," Steve told us.

The Ouija board dates back to 1890 and he had used the board with her many times when he was growing up. Victoria said it held a terrific energy so we were anxious to try it out.

After the opening prayer, we all placed our hands on the planchette, which began to move quite slowly. We got the letter *P*, but then Victoria was interrupted by the spirit of a young man who seemed to be very impatient.

"He worked as a runner here when it was a speakeasy or something, because all I keep getting is that this place was not what it seemed to be. It's like this building was in

Steve Fegley and his grandmother Meta's Ouija board.

two levels. Upstairs was business as usual and down here, there were things going on like money laundering and other illegal activities."

"He's about eighteen or nineteen, has black hair, and is telling me that he saw things that he wasn't supposed to see and was killed for that. Actually, he was tortured first because I hear him screaming. He is showing himself to me but he is unreachable because I think that the grisly events that lead up to his death literally drove him crazy."

Victoria asked if this young man could spell his name through the Ouija board, which spelled out the letters *P-O-R-Q* but then he began to fade out, only to be replaced by another man who she described as quite adamant.

"I think he's the leader of the many spirits who are down here," she told us. "He's a big man in stature and he's giving me the name *Frank*. I'm getting a very strong impression that he had something to do with the Mafia, and he really rules the rest of the spirits down here.

"He walks with a heavy step and can easily be heard, and I think, Marc, this is the spirit you heard outside your office. He was a businessman when he was alive and that's probably why he was coming into your office. I suspect he visits you quite often. He has a lot invested down here and he's still counting his money. In his world, time hasn't passed. He's in a world he created for himself and still sees things as they were. He coexists on another dimension."

Just then, the spirit of the man who Victoria picked up in the boiler room came through.

"I'm feeling a lot of pain in my jaw and back," said Victoria. "This man didn't die here, but he comes back because whatever precipitated the attack on him, I feel as though he was blindsided, and he's comes back here to try and wait for the men that attacked him. He's waiting to get justice. This goes back to the 1930s, I think. "There's also a woman here from the 1940s who is a very gentle spirit. It's interesting because there are a lot of gentle spirits down here, but also some that are truly crazy."

At that point, we tried again to see if any of them wanted to talk to us through the Ouija board, but were interrupted once again, this time by the presence of a little girl.

"Can you tell us your name by using the Ouija board?" Victoria asked.

The planchette slowly spelled out *P-E-R-I*, and then stopped between the letters *S* and *T*. The table then gave a shudder and the planchette moved to between the letters *G* and *H*.

When we asked for her age, the planchette moved to the number *8*, but we really weren't getting anything else that made any sense, so Victoria focused in mentally to communicate with her instead.

"She's telling me that she was brought here by a man and he molested, well, raped her. It was her mom's boyfriend who did it. It was 1923, and he did end up killing her."

Victoria then called upon help from the other side to assist the poor little soul's cross over to her mother, and at the same time, she let all the other spirits milling about know that they, too, could take the opportunity to cross over, if they so wished, and said that the door of light would remain open to any of them that wanted to do so at a later time.

No sooner had the words "door of light" left Victoria's mouth when all of a sudden a light went on in the room at the far end of the vault.

"That room had been dark all night," said Ginny, "but when I turned around and looked over there a second ago, the lights were on."

Even if the lights had been on sensors like some of the others in the basement, we were all sitting around the table, so there was nobody in that area to trip it.

As Barry walked over to that area with his camera to see if he could pick anything up, I clearly saw a small, wispy-like form whiz right past him and into that room, but he wasn't able to catch anything on film.

Thinking that it would be a great time to do some EVP work, Steve and I joined Barry and called out for a verbal response, but got no answer.

When we got back to the séance table, Victoria said that the atmosphere had suddenly gone flat and it was probably time to close the circle, even though she said she heard muffled voices coming from the room that was directly behind the vault.

After the closing prayer, we got up from the table and, just as we did, the light in the far room that had mysteriously turned on for us during the séance suddenly went out, as if to say, "That's all folks!"

Victoria and I then went around to the room where she heard the voices in the hopes that we'd be more successful in picking up EVP there.

While we didn't get anything on tape, Victoria did say she felt as though that was the room in which the little girl had been murdered because she picked up on the heavy residual energy emanating from one corner of the room.

As we were getting ready to leave, I called out and asked the entities if they would please give us all a sign of their presence before we left the basement…a kind of "one for the road" experience for us, but to my disappointment, nothing happened, so we decided to call it a night.

Because we had all gone to the bank in one vehicle, Barry and Victoria drove us back to my house where Ginny and Steve's car was parked.

After we were dropped off, the three of us where standing out on the sidewalk rehashing what had transpired that evening when, all of a sudden, I heard a loud voice that didn't belong to any of us emanating from somewhere close by. There wasn't anybody else with us but the voice kept on talking—and I realized that it was my voice we were hearing and it was coming from my purse.

As I unzipped the compartment where my digital recorder was, I heard myself saying, "If there's anyone here with us, could you please give us a sign of your presence? We really want to know that you are here."

The recorder was replaying the words I had spoken just before we left the bank. I knew that I had rewound the recorder and turned it off before we left, so we all found it strange that the DVR decided to turn itself on right then and cue itself up to repeat that particular phrase.

Even though I was disappointed that the spirits didn't comply with my request to make their presence known as we left the bank building, apparently someone must've heard me, followed us home and decided to give us a little belated surprise. It was quite unnerving, but better late than never, I suppose.

Note:

While there really isn't a lot written about the bank building, I did a little checking the next day about mob activity in Hollywood during the years that Victoria mentioned, and found that a man by the name of Frank DeSimone was the boss, or Don, of the Los Angeles Mafia from 1957 to 1967.

DeSimone was the son of Rosario "The Chief" DeSimone, who is said to have run Los Angeles with an iron fist until his death in 1946. Following his death, Jack Dragna became the new Don and used The Chief's son, Frank, a lawyer by trade, as the outfit's in-house legal consultant. Frank DeSimone, the next in line, became the new boss after Dragna succumbed to a fatal heart attack in 1956.

Frank became the third boss of the Los Angeles outfit of La Cosa Nostra and it's said that this colorful character was the inspiration for the *Godfather*'s lawyer-turned-mobster character, Tom Hagen, who was portrayed by Robert DuVall. It was said that DeSimone lived in fear his whole life of being assassinated. He wasn't always wrong about that. Joe Bonnano actually did plan to have him killed when he planned to overthrow the other five families in New York, but DeSimone managed to dodge the bullet and died of a heart attack in Downey, California on January 10, 1968.

Could this have been the Frank that joined us during our séance?

The Grey Ghost and Her Ghostly Inhabitants

"I am ready to meet my Maker. Whether my Maker is prepared for the great ordeal of meeting me is another matter."

—Winston Churchill

The *Queen Mary* is one of the last great Atlantic liners in existence. She was named after Queen Mary of Teck, the Queen consort of King George V and was launched on September 26th, 1934 by Her Majesty the Queen. During the launch ceremony, the Queen bestowed her name to the great ocean liner, known until then only as "Job Number 534."

Queen Mary herself was a staunch supporter of her husband and, after George's death in 1936, her eldest son, Edward, became King-Emperor. To Mary's dismay, he abdicated the same year in order to marry twice-divorced American socialite Mrs. Wallis Simpson. The Queen supported her second son, Albert, who succeeded to the throne as George VI and remained ruler until his death in 1952. George IV was the father of the current Queen of England, Elizabeth II.

The Queen took quite an interest in the upbringing of her granddaughters, Princesses Elizabeth and Margaret Rose, taking them on various excursions in London, to art galleries and museums. It is said that the Princesses' own parents thought it unnecessary for them to be taxed with any demanding educational regime.

She was known for setting the tone of the British Royal Family as a model of regal formality and propriety, especially during state occasions. She was the first Queen Consort to attend the coronation of her successors and is noted for superbly bejeweling herself for formal events. Queen Mary died in 1953 and left a collection of jewels now considered priceless.

The day of the ship's launching was quite festive and began with a quiet luncheon inside the confines of Buckingham Palace. Hours later, Queen Mary was presented with the belated birthday present of magnificent proportions. Stretching 1,018 feet in length and weighing more than 77,500 tons, the vessel was so large that the gigantic *Titanic* could have easily fit inside its hull with room to spare.

Throngs of spectators lined the shores of the river Clyde to witness the birth of one of Britain's greatest achievements. The Royal Marine Band played 'Rule Britannia' as she took off for the four-day crossing to the New World. Bookings for the Maiden Voyage from Southampton to New York City had been snapped up quickly and the passenger list read like a page from "Who's Who" as knights, ladies, dignitaries, and artists were escorted to their first-class suites.

During the launch ceremony, His Majesty, King George V said, "Now, with the hope of better trade on both sides of the Atlantic, let us look forward to her playing a great part in the revival of international commerce. It has been the nation's will that she should be completed, and today we can send her forth, ... a ship ... alive with beauty, energy and strength."

The first incident in what was to be an eventful career occurred just after the naming ceremony. On her way down the slipway, the ship began to run out of control. She hit the water far too fast and nearly flew straight across the River Clyde into the opposite bank. It appears that only pure luck allowed her drag chains to bring her to a stop before she ran aground. From then on, though, it was smooth sailing and four days later she arrived in New York.

The harbor was crowded with boats full of well-wishers and the curious. She was welcomed by thousands of Americans who couldn't wait to catch a glimpse of the already-famous liner. More than 100 journalists as well as representatives of the BBC and other networks were aboard to capture in print this landmark occasion. At the dock, 1,849 passengers and 1,186 officers and crew were offloaded and two stowaways were promptly returned to England.

The heyday of the *Queen Mary* were the years between 1936 and 1939 when she was the flagship of the Cunard White Star Line, and she soon captured the prized blue ribbon for a record-breaking crossing.

She was in the mid-Atlantic when Hitler invaded Poland on Friday, August 31, 1939. The following day, England and France declared war on Germany. Loaded with passengers and refugees, the ship's crew blacked out her portholes and the ship ran a zigzag course to elude submarines. She arrived safely in New York on Monday, September 4 and was immediately refitted as a troop ship which increased her capacity from 2,410 to 5,500.

Over the next six years, the ship carried troops to the war and British Prime Minister Winston Churchill to and from war conferences. She also transported several thousand German prisoners. During the war years, she visited places as far away as Bombay, India, Hong Kong, Rio de Janeiro, Brazil, and Sydney, Australia.

Churchill credited the ship with shortening the war by as much as a year and she was such a thorn in Hitler's side that he put a bounty on her: $250,000, and highest military honors to any captain who could sink her. No one ever collected.

After the war, she transported troops home and war brides and their babies from Britain to the United States and Canada, and was then converted back for passenger use.

Throughout the 1950s, the ship ran full most of the time, but by the end of the decade, regularly scheduled passenger plane flights were available across the North Atlantic, and almost overnight, massive transatlantic ocean liners became dinosaurs. By the mid 1960s, she was crossing the Atlantic carrying more crew than passengers, and since the ship was no longer profitable in her former capacity, Cunard offered her for sale in 1967.

The *Queen Mary* crossed the Atlantic Ocean 1,001 times before coming to permanent dock in Long Beach, California, when, in 1967, the ship was purchased as a tourist attraction, city icon, hotel, convention center, and museum. World-famous and loved by millions, the ship instantly put the City of Long Beach on the map. In 1992, friends of the *Queen Mary* permanently saved the ship for Long Beach and the world. The RMS Foundation, a non-profit organization, now manages the ship and intends to preserve her for display in Long Beach in perpetuity and hopes to return as much originality to the ship as possible.

She was called the *Grey Ghost* during her years as a World War II transport ship, but it wasn't until she docked in Long Beach that the *Queen Mary* became associated with the paranormal. Hundreds of apparitions have been reported, and since so many people had ghostly encounters, the owners set up special "Ghost Encounter" tours and a Paranormal Research Center.

Because the grand ocean liner hosted the world's rich and famous across the Atlantic, including the Duke and Duchess of Windsor, Greta Garbo, David Niven, Mary Pickford, and George and Ira Gershwin, visitors who spend the night at the Hotel Queen Mary can easily imagine themselves on a transatlantic journey rubbing elbows with these famous folks, and a few of the overnight guests actually have been in the company of famous personalities—in a paranormal sort of way.

The stateroom where Winston Churchill stayed is said to be particularly haunted. According to legend, he planned the D-Day invasion while taking a bath and playing with toy ships in this room. People who stay there often report smelling his cigar smoke.

During her sixty-year history, the *Queen Mary* was the site of forty-nine reported deaths, so there are plenty of potential spirits to haunt her hallways and staterooms. Hauntings include a young crewman in the engine room, swimmers in the first-class pool, a man in black, and a woman in blue roaming the ship. One guide attributed the woman in blue haunting to reports of a woman being raped in one of the tiny rooms.

Another frequently seen apparition is that of one of the ship's former officers. Senior 2nd Officer William Stark was accidentally poisoned in 1949, when he drank tetrachloride that the staff captain kept in an old gin bottle. This uniformed seaman is often found wandering the decks.

Located fifty feet below water level is the engine room, which is said to be a hotbed of paranormal activity. The room's infamous "Door 13" crushed at least two men to death at different times during the ship's history. The most recent death was that of an eighteen-year-old crew member who was crushed to death in 1966 during a routine watertight door drill. Dressed in blue coveralls and sporting a beard, the young man has often been spied walking the length of Shaft Alley before disappearing at the site where he met his painful demise.

As his sad story goes, on July 10, 1966, a fireman named John Peddar was participating in a drill where the watertight doors were sealed on the ship. Unfortunately, he was unable to get out of the doorway in time and was crushed by the massive force.

Since the horrible accident, there have been numerous reports of John's ghost in the engine room. One sighting came on August 13, 1991 while a couple was participating in a tour of the ship. Having heard the story, the man jokingly asked, "John Peddar, would you like to join us?" He and his wife laughed and proceeded through the watertight door and up the stairs. Almost immediately, they sensed that they were not alone. They turned to look back at the doorway and the man then felt something brush across his face.

The couple didn't think too much of the experience until they were safely outside and the wife noticed that the husband had grease on his face on the spot where something had brushed against him earlier. Grease was abundant in the engine room back when the ship was operational, but it is very unlikely that a tourist would come in contact with any today. What's more, neither one of them had grease on their hands or anywhere else on their bodies. They believe that the ghost of John Peddar decided to take them up on their offer.

Two more popular spots for the Queen's otherworldly guests are its first and second class swimming pools.

Though neither are utilized today for their original purpose, some spirits don't seem to be aware of that. In the first-class swimming pool, which has been closed for more than three decades, ghostly women have often been seen wearing 1930s-style swimming suits and wandering the decks near the pool. Other people have reported the sounds of splashing and have seen wet footprints leading from the deck to the changing rooms. It must be noted at this point that the pool is completely dry.

In the second-class poolroom, the spirit of a little girl named Jackie has often been seen and heard. The unfortunate girl supposedly drowned in the pool during the ship's sailing days and reputedly refused to move on. Her voice, as well as the sounds of laughter, have been captured here.

In the Queen's Salon, which once served as the ship's first-class lounge, a beautiful young woman in an elegant white evening gown has often been seen dancing alone in the shadows of the corner of the room.

More odd occurrences have been witnessed in a number of first-class staterooms. Here, reports have been made of a tall dark-haired man appearing in a 1930s-style suit, as well as water running, lights turning on in the middle of the night, and phones ringing in the early morning hours with no one on the other end of the line.

In the third-class children's playroom, a baby's cry has often been heard, which is thought to be an infant boy who died shortly after his birth. Leigh Travers Smith is said to have died a few hours after birth, but not without heroic attempts by ship's surgeons to save his life. There have been reports that late at night a baby's cry can be heard from the room. Other phenomenon occurring throughout the ship are the sounds of distinct knocks, doors slamming and high pitched squeals, drastic temperature changes, and the aromas of smells long past.

The boiler room was probably the most dangerous area on the ship during its operation. One unfortunate crew learned just how deadly the boiler room could be when several pipes containing high-pressure steam exploded, killing several of them.

After the *Queen Mary* was permanently berthed in Long Beach, California, the boiler room was gutted out completely. Regardless of this fact, many ghostly sightings have been reported in that area and paranormal activity still occurs in that locale to this day.

Another reportedly haunted spot is the Promenade Deck near the passenger information booth. The sighting was made by two employees who were working at the booth. While carrying out their daily tasks, a strange woman caught their attention. She was attired in clothing from the late '30s and appeared a bit blurry around the edges. The employees watched as she walked down the hallway, and as she approached a pillar, she stepped behind it, out of their view. When one of the employees walked over to the pillar, they were surprised to see that no one was there. The woman had completely vanished.

With all the reported sightings on board, the *RMS Queen Mary* has attracted many psychics in recent years, some of which have conducted séances to find out who some of the ship's ghosts might be.

The infamous Door 13.

Richard Senate Speaks With Hollywood Royalty

Paranormal investigator Richard Senate is recognized as an expert on ghosts and hauntings. He is the author of fifteen books on the subject and has visited over 230 haunted houses all over the USA and UK.

A couple of years ago, Richard organized a séance on the *Queen Mary*. His wife, psychic Debbie Christenson Senate, conducted the séance.

"The *Queen Mary* is a very haunted ship," says Richard. "Our séance was held in the forward meeting room near the bow of the ship and lots of strange things happened, including a door that opened and closed by itself. We were at the table, the door opened, then I said as a joke, "Who ever you are, please come in and join us at the circle.

"At that point the door closed. It was locked. The spirit was linked to Hollywood's past. This is the transcription of that event:

Question: Who are you? (*Richard asked the entranced Debbie*)

Answer: Alan. My name is Alan Mo Pree. Don't you know me?

Question: Why should I know you?

Answer: I'm a star in the moving pictures. I've been in over 200 films.

Question: Were you in any movies we might have seen?

Answer: I think so—I was in *The King and I* and *My Darling Clementine*. I was in a lot of pictures.

Question: Why are you on board the Queen Mary?

Answer: I'm going home Old Boy. Back to London. I always go on the *Queen*. But, I must tell you that this ship isn't going fast enough. It's taking far too long to reach the UK. Someone needs to speak with the captain.

Question: Do you know the ship isn't moving?

Answer: It's a bit slow, that's all.

Question: When did you come to Hollywood?

Answer: It was 1923. I came out to make silent pictures, and just stayed on. I met some of the great ones, too. Charlie Chaplin. He was a master of comedy. Keaton was greater though. It came naturally to him. He never had to work for a laugh, it was all part of his nature. Charlie had to work for everything he ever had. If he would have been able to keep his mouth shut, he might still be in the States making films today.

Question: Did you know any of the other big names?

Answer: I knew them all.

Question: Did you ever meet Errol Flynn?

Answer: We used to go clubbing together. He drank like a fish you know. He was a charming fellow though—for an Aussie, you know.

Question: Was he Gay?

Answer: He was always happy, especially around the ladies.

Question: I mean, was he a homosexual?

Answer: I head those stories. He wasn't that way. The ladies liked him too much and he liked them. Anything in a skirt it was. He liked them young and pretty when sober and anyway when he was drunk. I once saw him with this hatcheck girl who must have been older than.... (*laughter*) No, he didn't look at men in that way.

Question: Did you know John Wayne?

Answer: The cowboy? I met Tom Mix once and he was a great man.

Question: Did you know others, Bogart? Bob Hope?

"At this point, the séance became a diatribe denouncing a fellow named Samson who Alan said was a warlock and had caused his career to falter. Lastly, the spirit asked for gin and tonic and was gone.

"Research indicated there was a British actor named Alan Mowbray who played the sea captain on the Film *The King and I*. By all accounts, he did like a drink now and again in life. Maybe more research could discover the identity of Samson, the witch, and why Alan hated him so much."

For those not familiar with the British actor, Alan Mowbray appeared in dozens of films during his career, including *The King and I* and *Clementine,* and was one of the founding members of the Screen Actors Guild. In later years, he appeared on a number of American television shows including, *The Man From U.N.C.L.E., The Beverly Hillbillies, The Flying Nun,* and *The Patty Duke Show.* Lovers of ghostly film comedies might recall Mowbray's turns as the long-suffering butler in the first two *Topper* films and as "the Devil Himself" (as he was billed). Mowbray died of a heart attack in 1969. No reference to a warlock named Samson could be found.

Victoria Gross' Haunted Tour

Psychic Victoria Gross has worked as a ghost tour guide on the *Queen Mary*, so I was curious about her own personal experiences on the ship. She says,

"Many believe the *Queen Mary* to be haunted, while others dismiss any claims of the supernatural. From my experience as a tour guide on the Paranormal Shipwalk, and that of others who have been on the tours or have rented rooms from the ship's hotel, I would say that there is good evidence leaning towards ghostly encounters. Disembodied voices, misty apparitions, the sound of footsteps with no explainable reason are just some of the paranormal phenomena that continue to occur on board the ship."

B Deck

Victoria continues,

"I was leading a group down the hall on the port side of B Deck coming away from the Isolation Ward when all of a sudden I heard someone say 'hey' in a whispered voice. I turned to the woman behind me and asked if she said anything to me; she said 'no.' Looking at the two men behind her, I saw that their eyes were as big as saucers and they excitedly stated that they had also heard the voice."

The Swimming Pool

"On the upper deck of the first-class swimming pool, I saw what appeared to be an apparition starting to form. It did not form completely and was gone within seconds. The torso area was of a white mist, and from the waist down, the color of sky blue was prominent. Was this the spirit of the little girl they call Jackie? Many have seen a child spirit with a sky-blue dress in this pool area.

"It's reported that Jackie has often been seen and heard in this area. The unfortunate child is said to have drowned in the pool during the ship's sailing days and reputedly refuses to move on. Her voice, as well as the sounds of laughter, have been captured here many times.

"Some people claim that the changing rooms located in the first-class swimming pool area contain a vortex.

"A vortex is considered to be an area where energy is heavily condensed and acts as a doorway to other dimensions allowing spirits to pass through. A vortex may be geographically created by ley lines such as those found at Stonehenge in England and Sedona, Arizona, or may appear for no apparent reason.

"Is there really a vortex in the changing rooms? I am not sure, though that does not negate the amount of paranormal activity that many have encountered in this area.

"One night, as a group of us walked into the rooms, we heard loud banging noises and audible voices. Many times while standing quite still in the changing stalls, we could hear someone walking on the upper deck of the pool area. Checking with the security officer that accompanies us, we found that no one but us was in that location and the door had been locked preventing anyone else from entering.

"On another evening when I was in one of the stalls, I heard a constant scuffling sound on the flood behind me. At first I thought it was my assistant, Andrew, who was in the stall with me, until he mentioned that he heard the same noise coming from behind him. Could it have been an animal? When we turned on the light, there was nothing there.

The haunted changing rooms.

The Forward Cargo Hold

According to historical accounts, on October 2, 1942, the *Queen Mary* accidentally sank one of her escorts, slicing through the light cruiser HMS *Curacoa* (D41), with the loss of 338 lives. Due to the constant danger of being attacked by U-Boats, the *Queen Mary* could not stop, or even slow down, to rescue survivors. Forty years later, a television crew left their audio recorder running overnight in the exact location where the two ships collided. As the tape played back the next day, incredible sounds of pounding could be heard. Others have claimed to hear voices and blood-curdling noises from the same area.

Victoria adds,

"Once the tour is situated in the bowels of the ship, the gate located four decks above is locked to prevent intruders.

Orbs below deck.

As we stand in semi-darkness, we hear heavy footsteps from the deck above. Security officer Ivan checks the source of the disturbance and always comes back reporting that no one is there. These accounts are just a few in a list of occurrences that have been witnessed by many in that area."

The Isolation Ward

"The first time I entered the Isolation Ward was in 2003. Then, as now, I find it to be one of the creepiest places on the ship. It was used to isolate passengers who were found to be suffering from communicable diseases while on board the ship and the ward was also where stowaways were held.

"My initial visit revealed the same impressions I receive to this day—that of a young man who is mentally insane. To be honest, I do not believe it to be the actual

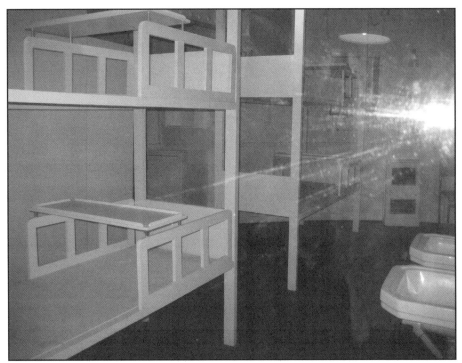

The Isolation Ward—Reflections or spirit?

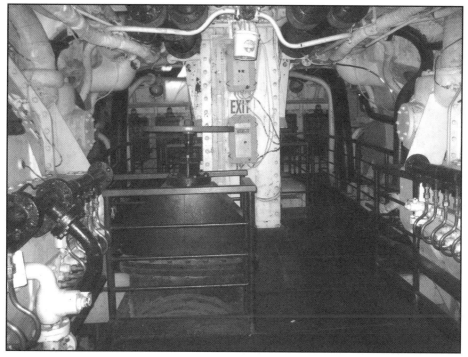

The Engine Room.

spirit of the man, just an imprint, what is called residual haunting. This is like watching a video tape playing the same scene over and over again.

It is where the spirit leaves an imprint onto the etheric field of the earth. Since it is not the actual spirit we are seeing, but just their impression, we cannot communicate with it or it with us. Even though there is no contact, we still can read the impressions from the psychic atmosphere surrounding it."

Victoria advises,

"There is no guarantee that one will meet the acquaintance of a specter on any ghost tour. Ghosts are like people; they are unpredictable and will show up when they please, but on *The Queen Mary*, they do show up quite a bit."

Kenny Kingston Still Talks To...

Now about those ghosts. I'm sure they're here and I'm not half so alarmed at meeting up with any of them as I am at having to meet the live nuts I have to see every day.

—Former First Lady Bess Truman

Psychic to the Stars Kenny Kingston has been talking to Hollywood stars, both living and in the hereafter, for many years. The celebrated psychic has a client list that rivals *Who's Who* and includes Marilyn Monroe, Greta Garbo, U. S. Presidents Truman and Eisenhower, Hugh Jackman, John Wayne, the Duke and Duchess of Windsor, and Princess Diana.

I've known Kenny for well over thirty years, and he never ceases to amaze me. He's a kind and gentle soul with a tremendous sense of humor, and over time, he's taught me quite a bit about the spirit world and about my connection to it as well.

For years he has chided me about not developing my psychic ability to its full potential. We are all born with that ability but it needs to be nurtured. At first, I think I was always too afraid to "kick it up a notch," but when I did start to let down the wall, things really did begin to happen. Thank God Kenny was there to help me sort them out.

A couple of years ago, I was lying in bed and out of nowhere, I heard loud a male voice say, "They're trying to kill Judy."

The only Judy I knew was my friend Jenette's mother, who at the time was in the hospital following back surgery. I was frightened by the message so the next morning I was on the phone to Kenny. I was actually hoping that he'd say I had imagined the voice, but Kenny assured me that what I heard was an urgent plea from spirit. He strongly suggested that I call Jenette and pass on the message, which I did.

Because Jenette lives out of state, she wasn't privy to the daily goings on with her mother's care, which was being handled by her sisters, and there wasn't a great deal she could do. What she did eventually find out after her mother unexpectedly passed away several weeks later, was that while Judy was recuperating in a nursing care facility, she was being severely overmedicated with three different anti-depression drugs which might well have lead to her untimely demise.

Another message came to me a few weeks later when I heard what sounded like a young female voice say, "I died quickly in the accident." I was a nervous wreck until I was able to call up my friends the next morning and determine that they were all still alive and well.

When I asked Kenny why I keep getting singled out to receive such messages, he explained that people with strong psychic ability put out a sort of beacon to the spirit world, and sometimes, when the spirit of someone on the other side has a message to relay, they are drawn to us, whether it's about someone we know, like in Judy's case, or it's just from someone who has something they need to tell someone, as was the case with the mysterious female who contacted me about her passing. (That mystery might have been solved when I was involved in a séance that took place at Boardner's Bar in Hollywood. I've written about it in the Boardner's chapter further along in the book, so you be the judge. Meanwhile, back to Kenny.)

I recently asked Kenny who his favorite person to speak to on the other side was, and he said, "Well, of course that would be my mother, and my grandfather, Henry C. He was the one who got me through school. He's one of my guides and I'm always pleased that he's still with me, but I'm always happy for any spirit who takes the time to come to me. That's the important thing because they all have busy schedules doing something on the other side in their new lives and have to take time out to come back to me."

Kenny's glass-walled home in Studio City, overlooking the San Fernando Valley area of Southern California is filled with memorabilia from his many celebrity clients and friends. He has a jeweled throne chair from Broadway and film actor Clifton Webb, a crystal candelabra and table and chairs from Marilyn Monroe, a silver candle holder from Tallulah Bankhead, a gold picture frame from the Duchess of Windsor, handspun pottery from Sir Noel Coward, object d'art from Greta Garbo, and a potpourri of other fascinating items—gifts from the great and the near great.

Throughout his career, Kenny has been giving readings to people from all walks of life, but he is most famous for his association with celebrities, both here and in spirit. In his best-selling book, *I Still Talk To...* Kenny conducted a number of Hollywood séances to get in touch with some of his former friends and clients and see how they are doing on the Other Side. He says they really enjoy the opportunity to communicate once again with those of us on the "Earthplane" and for the chance to relay messages to their fans or loved ones; perhaps to finish some unfinished business or say things they might not have had the chance to say while they were alive. Often times, they bring us up to date on what their "lives" are like now in the spirit world.

Mae West

Mae West was a dear friend of Kenny's mother, Kaye, a lovely woman who was born the seventh daughter of a seventh daughter. Kaye taught Kenny all she knew about psychic ability, and it was Mae West, who was very in tune with the spirit world herself, who encouraged Kenny to develop the art of clairaudio (listening to the sound of a voice and picking up psychic vibrations from it) when he was just seven years old. Kenny and Mae remained good friends throughout her lifetime and continue that cherished friendship even now.

During a séance conducted at Kingston's home while he was writing *I Still Talk to...*, Mae's spirit came through easily to both Kenny and his associate, Valerie Porter, who were the only participants.

A red candle was lit, and because Mae used to recline on a chaise lounge while contacting spirits and dictating material to stenographers, Kenny thought it would be a good idea to lie down on his orange velvet loveseat, thus striking a position that Mae would be comfortable with.

Soon the candle began to flicker and Kenny's breathing became heavy, and he felt a bit lightheaded, indicating that he was entering a trance state. A white mist seemed to seep in through the front door, and then took on the shape of a person who floated over to Kenny. The mist seemed to enfold the psychic and hovered over him for a moment or so, then broke into tiny particles and scattered. Kenny mumbled, rolled his head from side to side, then spoke in a distinctive feminine voice.

"I just came back from a walk," said the entity. "I like to walk here on the other side as much as I did at my beach house in Santa Monica. Walkin' kept me in shape, ya know."

Although he didn't know who might actually come through when the séance began, it became clear that this was definitely the familiar voice of his friend Mae West.

Sometimes spirit communications are difficult, but Mae's spirit was strong and she had quite a bit to say about her life on the other side.

She explained that while she has had several incarnations on the earthplane over time, people on the other side immediately recognize her as Mae West. She also admitted that she still has an interest in entertainment and gets up and does a few songs now and then, sharing the ethereal stage with the likes of Cole Porter, Jeanette McDonald and Nelson Eddy and other late greats, but she told Kenny and Valerie that she also spends a great deal of time in the capacity of a "greeter," welcoming new souls who have recently passed over.

"When a person's life is taken suddenly or brutally," says Kenny, explaining just what a greeter does, "that person's loved ones in spirit may not be alerted to the passing right away, and in these cases, a committee, or greeter, may be assigned to a spirit. This is either a friendly soul or a group of souls who are sent to comfort and guide the newcomer until their loved ones have been notified and are ready to provide comfort themselves."

"There was nothin' I liked better'n my public comin' up to me and sayin', 'Hello, Miss West, glad to see ya', so now, I go to see them." She continued, "See, they come here to the other side and they're kinda groggy and need rest. So as they're restin', I'll sit with 'em and meditate over 'em, visualizin' 'em waking up strong and healthy. Then they open their eyes and it's kinda surprisin' to 'em. They'll say, 'Why, you're Mae West!' and I say, 'That's right, dearie!'"

For many departed souls, having Mae West as the first person they see immediately after they cross over definitely brings new meaning to the old saying, "I've died and gone to heaven."

During the rest of their time together, Mae talked more about life on the other side.

She explained that being comfortable in the afterlife is a matter of perception. "You make up your mind that you're going to be comfortable here and you can be," she explained. "Ya create what ya want in your mind."

To better explain, she use used the late great composer Cole Porter as an example.

"Cole Porter sits down at the piano and we get some lovely tunes outta him. Now let me tell ya, this is kind of strange. He sits at what you'd think would be a piano, and goes through the motions using his fingers, ya know, but ya don't actually see the piano. It ain't in front of him!"

"Some people swear they see a piano, like they swear they see tables and chairs and beds. I don't see any of it; they just kinda "sense" them and know they're there. It's not real furniture like you know it. The thing is, you don't *need* a chair, you can feel relaxed and feel the *sensation* of a chair. You want to lie down? You automatically feel the sensation of a bed. It's gonna look like whatever you create in your mind."

Mae also offered several predictions about life here on Earth in the twenty-first century including a cure for diabetes which will be in the offing by the year 2020. She also talked about reincarnation and explained that it's a matter of choice whether or not a soul wants to come back and live another life or not.

"We can go to classes to learn how to get born again, and they tell us about upcomin' chances, then ya decide whether ya think that would be a good life for the lessons ya'd like to learn next time and kinda put in an application."

Mae said that while she does plan to reincarnate some time in the future, it won't be for quite a while because she still has lots of things yet to do on the other side.

"I got no complaints here. We don't know what sickness or tiredness is and I don't spend a lot of time thinking of what might have been. It's 'Paradiso" to me and I love it."

Marilyn Monroe

Kenny was Marilyn Monroe's one and only psychic and he spoke to her just four days before her passing. At the time, he found her to be in good spirits and she was looking forward to resuming her work on the film *Something's Got To Give*, a remake of *My Favorite Wife*. The new version starred Marilyn, Dean Martin, and Cyd Charisse. Prior to starting work on the film, Monroe had been absent from the screen for over a year. She had recently undergone gallbladder surgery, and had dropped over twenty-five pounds, reaching the lowest weight of her adult life.

On the first day of production, April 23, 1962, Monroe telephoned producer Henry Weinstein to tell him that she had a severe sinus infection and would not be on the set that morning. Apparently, she had caught the infection after a trip to New York City during which she had visited her acting coach, Lee Strasberg of The Actors Studio, to go over her upcoming role. Over the next month, production continued mostly without Monroe and eventually the studio decided to replace the actress with Lee Remick, but Dean Martin, who had leading lady approval said, "No Marilyn, no picture." The project seemingly ended there.

Then, realizing they had thrown $2 million away, Fox decided to re-hire Monroe. They agreed to pay her more than her previous salary of $100,000; however she had to agree to make two more films for Fox. She accepted the offer on the condition that director George Cukor be replaced with Jean Negulesco, who had directed her in *How to Marry a Millionaire*.

On August 1, 1962, Marilyn called Kenny and asked if he'd like to go to the beach with her, but as he had a full day's work ahead of him, he had to decline and suggested that she dress down so she wouldn't be recognized and go alone. Marilyn called him that evening and said she had a wonderful time. They chatted for a while, and just before hanging up, she told him, "I love everyone right now, Kenny. And you know, love is the one immortal thing about us; without love, what else can life mean?"

"Those words will echo through my ears for the rest of my life," says Kenny, "because they were the last words Marilyn ever spoke to me while she was alive."

Because Kingston had communicated with his dear friend several times since her passing, he felt confident that she would appear once again when he began writing his book and his confidence was not misplaced.

The séance was held at The Cinegrill in The Hollywood Roosevelt Hotel, a place that Monroe was quite familiar with. She lived at the hotel for a couple of years during the early part of her career, and Marilyn's mirror, a fixture in the hotel lobby where people see Marilyn's ghost on a regular basis, is one of Hollywood's most famous attractions. The mirror was originally housed in one of the hotel bungalows next to the pool which was her favorite room.

When the séance took place, Kenny was performing at the Cinegrill and was staying in a suite on the tenth floor. One afternoon, while he was in the shower preparing to go downstairs for a rehearsal, he heard a familiar voice say, "I'll be down there."

Following a run-through of his performance and after everyone else had left, Kenny and Valerie closed all the doors and windows in the Cinegrill, sat down at an intimate table in the center of the room and turned out the lights.

It wasn't long before they felt a slight chill in the room, a sure sign that spirit was trying to enter. Kenny believes that music helps raise the vibrations and is especially important prior to spirit contact so he and Valerie began to sing two of his favorite hymns, *In the Garden* and *Only Believe*.

They were midway through the first hymn when the cold air grew stronger and the breeze enveloped them. Then, they heard a familiar voice, barely a whisper at first, coming from the direction of the stage that said, "Hello, it's me!"

There was a strong scent of perfume in the air, which felt as though it was charged with electricity. Then a tiny dot of light resembling a spotlight formed on the stage, then expanded into a white glow.

"Slowly, a white gown appeared and then golden hair," said Kenny, "and finally, an angelic face." Marilyn Monroe had arrived.

During their session, a happy, carefree Marilyn told Kenny that she was quite happy on the other side and was studying philosophy and psychology, explaining that she always wanted to be an intellectual. "You know, I married Arthur Miller because he was an intellectual. I found that very sexy." She also admitted that she had married Miller for the wrong reasons. "He was nice enough to me," she said, "but he was not the right man for me. I could never be 'smart enough' with Arthur."

When the subject came around to that fateful evening of Marilyn's passing, she was adamant that her death was not the result of a murder or an intentional suicide.

"I didn't kill myself! Happy—I was happy! I was working again. I was starting a new picture, but I was just so tired—I never meant to take so many pills. It was an accident."

And then, answering a burning question before it was even asked, Marilyn stated, "They weren't part of it!" referring to the common speculation that the Kennedys might have been involved in her demise. "It was an accident," she insisted, and then also dismissed claims that she was involved with Robert F. Kennedy. "I never—*not ever*—had an affair with Robert Fitzgerald Kennedy! He was a family man!"

Marilyn then went on to tell Kenny that she did have plans to reincarnate, but the next rime around, she would be coming back as a man. "Men used me before as Norma Jean and Marilyn, but I learned to use them, too. I learned to give Marilyn Monroe's body to get Marilyn Monroe something in return."

"I'll be a very good male," she laughed. "Because I'll be sensitive. I'll treat women the way they should be treated, with respect and dignity, but I won't be coming back for quite a while," she continued, "because I'm watching over Melanie Griffith. I want to help her to be strong."

President Harry Truman

I recently asked Kenny if there were any spirits he'd particularly like to speak to again and his immediate answer was Harry Truman.

"I only saw him on two occasions, but he was very down to earth and had a tremendous sense of humor," Kenny recalls.

Kenny's first meeting with the late President was in San Francisco many years ago when then-president Truman, who had taken over the office after FDR passed away, was in the Northern California city running for "reelection."

Kenny was in his office one afternoon when the phone rang and the voice on the other end voice said, "Harry Truman here. I want to talk to the spirits."

At first, Kenny thought it might be a joke until two men wearing earphones appeared at his door a few minutes later and said, "We're ready to go to the President," and off they all went.

Three years later they met again, this time at the Waldorf Astoria Hotel in New York City. During that meeting, Truman spoke about the White House ghosts.

"You know, I listen to the 'ghosts' walk around the hallways in the White House, but they don't frighten me," he told Kenny. "In fact, when they rattle the windows or move the drapes back and forth, I just smile and invite them right on in."

He also mentioned the fact that he was planning to build the Truman Library in Independence, Missouri, where he hoped to be buried.

"I kind of like the idea," he told Kenny, "because I just might want to get up now and then and stroll in my office there."

President Truman passed away on December 26, 1972, and was indeed buried in the courtyard of the Truman Library in Independence.

While one never has expectations about who might want to come through during a séance, Kenny was delighted to have an ethereal visit from Harry Truman when he was working on *I Still Talk To...*

During that forty-five minute session, Mr. Truman spoke candidly about ex-presidents Nixon, Bush, Reagan, and Clinton, the fact that he has no regrets about the decisions he made as President, and about the state of our country which, at the time, he felt was in bad shape.

"I told Bess the other day, 'What's wrong with the United States now?' The President's guarded by the highest amount of security possible and that's fine, but four blocks from the White House, there are bars on people's windows they're so afraid. Every man, woman, and child should be able to walk the streets without fear of robbery, murder, or attack."

"Balance the budget—put American people first," he continued. "Buy American, sell American. No person should be homeless or hungry. I love this country. Good night and God Bless America."

And with those parting words, he was gone.

"President Truman was very down-to-earth and had a very spiritual side," says Kenny. "He didn't have a big ego, but had lots of determination."

Greta Garbo

One day I asked Kenny if he had a favorite celebrity spirit he was always happy to see, and he said that he always enjoys talking to Greta Garbo. "She was so elusive in life, and now that she comes back, she's free. She's like a free spirit. She comes back and can speak her mind and not carry a facade, but just be the real Miss G. She was a legend, a true phenomenon, and I am honored to have known her."

During one recent séance, Miss Garbo touched on the subject of suicide and passed on an interesting bit of information about what happens to people who take their own lives once they get to the other side.

Using actor Charles Boyer as an example, she told Kenny and Valerie that Boyer was there on the *Other Side*, but was resting, like in a very deep, deep sleep and was barely able to open his eyes. Since Boyer passed away in 1978, Valerie asked if such a long, drawn out rest was normal.

"It certainly can be," said Miss G through Kenny. "There's no time in the spirit world so the year someone passed is relatively unimportant. It's an individual process of waking up and progressing. But overdoses, whether suicidal or not, take a very long time to adjust. After all—it was not that person's time to go. They tampered with nature and the Master's will and plan for them. Their presence in the spirit world is unplanned, and it's like trying to get into a posh restaurant without a reservation, so the spirit is in limbo or at rest until the timing is right."

In his book, Kenny also gave the reason why his good friend Miss Garbo got the reputation for being such a recluse.

"Greta Garbo suffered from both claustrophobia and agoraphobia," Kenny explains. "It took me a long time to convince her of this, but she'd sometimes feel claustrophobic indoors as if the walls were closing in on her and she'd have to get out and walk. Yet at other times, when she did get out, she was terrified. She panicked and literally froze at the sight of people. It wasn't that she didn't want to talk to people. She simply couldn't."

So therein lies the answer to one of the mysteries surrounding the mysterious Greta Garbo. She didn't really 'want to be alone'; she just couldn't help it.

Whether he's writing books, giving interviews, or just sitting around the house, the spirits of the immortals always seem to come through.

As we were winding up our conversation, I asked Kenny who he would like to speak to that he hadn't been able to contact as yet, and after a moment's thought, he said, "Probably Cary Grant. I read something funny about him the other day in which he once said, 'Everyone wants to be Cary Grant. Even I want to be Cary Grant.'"

When I asked Kenny if he had been a big fan of the actor, he responded by saying, "I liked his debonair manner, and his style of clothing. You see," he explained with a laugh, "we had the same tailor for a very long time."

Dearly Departed's Possessed (?) Possessions

"From ghoulies and ghosties and long-leggedy beasties and things that go bump in the night, Good Lord, deliver us!"

Scottish prayer

Where the *possessed possessions* are kept.

ollywood historian and owner of Dearly Departed Tours, Scott Michaels, is well known in Hollywood as a Master of the Macabre. He's a walking encyclopedia of where the rich and famous died and how they met their makers.

Scott's three-hour "Tragical History Tour" takes passengers to such infamous locations as The Manson Murders site, the "last gasp locations" of Frank Sinatra, William Frawley, River Phoenix, Dee Dee Ramone, and Bela Lugosi. The REAL Nightmare on Elm Street house (The Menendez home, where Lyle and Eric Menendez brutally murdered their parents) is also included as well as Paramount/RKO Studios, Mae West's last home, and many other interesting and often grisly locations. There are almost 100 sites visited, and all the while, Scott narrates through decades of death and murder, reporting on the most tickling tales of Tinseltown tragedies.

"I've been interested in death since I was a tyke," says Scott, "My mother recalls taking me to a funeral of a young family member when I was three years old. On the way to the grave site, I noticed the tent set up, and asked, 'Mom, are we going to the circus?' I suppose in a way, we were.

"Growing up in Detroit, I lived on one of the most dangerous intersections in the city. Fatal accidents were normal. There was a family ritual when we were jarred awake from our slumber by that horrible noise of a car accident outside. One of us would call the police, another would grab the towels, etc. One night, while I was asleep, a car hit a lamp post in front of our house. I heard the sound of slamming brakes, the impact, and the live wires of a fallen street light zapping away. I got out of bed, looked out the window, yawned, and returned to bed. You get the idea.

"Eventually, I tired of circling the bowl of Detroit and made my way to Chicago, where I started my company, "Dearly Departed," specializing in dead celebrity memorabilia like key chains, T-shirts, etc., adorned with tombstone photographs. It was also then that I became fanatic about tracking down my favorite celebrity graves. It was natural that I hooked up with Greg Smith and his famous Grave Line Tours in Hollywood."

Scott became Grave Line's "Director of Undertaking" and remained with the firm until its unfortunate demise a few years later. It was about the same time that Scott fell in love and moved to England. He was there for five years before returning to the States. Once back, he kind of picked up where he left off and created Dearly Departed Tours.

As the business grew, so did Scott's credibility as an expert on Hollywood deaths and he's been featured on dozens of televisions shows, in newspaper and magazine articles, and is a regular on Liza Gibbons' radio show, *Hollywood Confidential*.

In addition to Dearly Departed, Scott also has his own web site, findadeath.com. One of the features of the site is his selection of dead celebrity memorabilia that is for sale. Interested shoppers can buy stones taken from the exact spot where Patsy Cline's body was found, a piece of John Denver's death plane, and many more gruesome items. Along with the sale items, Scott has quite a few personal bits of celebrity memorabilia that he keeps at home.

A little over a year ago, shortly after moving into a new apartment, he began to notice some strange disturbances. Something (or someone) kept waking him up in the middle of the night. He'd see a black shape hovering over his bed on a regular basis and over time the phenomenon intensified. Not being a "ghost person" he was at a loss for what to do. I suggested he "sage" the apartment, but that did no good.

A few months later, a well-known psychic took one of his tours and they got to talking. Scott mentioned the fact that he thought he was being haunted and she offered to come by to check it out. After a quick investigation of the apartment, it was determined that Scott's unusual collection, which includes such items as a piece of Jayne Mansfield's heart-shaped swimming pool and many house bricks from her home (which has since been demolished,) bricks that came out of the fireplace at the site of the infamous Manson murders, tiles from the pool where Brian Jones drowned, a piece of the letter *H* from the original Hollywood sign where actress Peg Entwistle committed suicide, and some bricks from the now-defunct Ambassador Hotel along with a piece of linoleum from the hotel pantry where Robert Kennedy's head hit the ground right after he was shot, could very well be the reason for the disturbances.

The psychic suggested that Scott move some of the items out of the living room and into another area of the apartment, which he did, and the phenomenon did then settle down, but since the "collectibles" are still under the same roof, he was still uneasy.

Going on that assumption, I thought it might be a good idea to do a more thorough investigation of the place, and if we found anything out of the ordinary, we would conduct a séance to see who might still be hanging around. It should also be mentioned at this point that Scott's apartment is directly across the street from the very haunted Paramount Studios and just down the block from Hollywood Forever Cemetery.

Both the studio and Hollywood Forever have the reputation for being quite haunted, and a great many of their ghosts belong to celebrities. Apparitions have been seen floating in and out of the walls that surround the properties, so it makes sense that some might venture out into the neighborhood as well. Perhaps Scott and his collection were acting as a beacon to draw them in.

I assembled our "team" of paranormal investigators, Victoria Gross and Barry Conrad, and set a date to do the investigation.

At first, Scott had some reservations about doing a séance at his house because he was afraid we might leave some unwanted spirits behind after we left, but we assured him that wouldn't be the case, and because he really wanted to find out if his collection was responsible for the disturbances, the pros outweighed the cons.

When we arrived at the apartment a few nights later, we found his home to be as warm and inviting as our host and although Victoria did pick up on a few spirits that were milling about, the atmosphere wasn't the least bit negative.

We were all immediately drawn to Scott's large display case where many of the suspicious items are kept. When Scott opened it up, Victoria said that she felt an immediate rush of energy, but explained that it was merely residual energy rather than spirit-made.

With haunted objects, the stronger the emotional energy attached to an object, the more likely it will be to display paranormal behavior, and how an object is used, created, cared for or abused, plus the material it is made from, all contribute to the potential for hosting spirit energy. Every object is capable of holding an imprint that may or may not be a happy one.

In many cases, after a person's death they continue to be attached mentally to favorite objects of theirs from when they

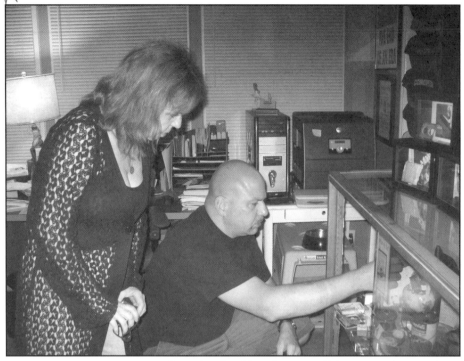

Scott showing Victoria some of his possessed possessions.

were alive. Their spirits loiter around items such as a favorite chair, piece of jewelry, or perhaps even an old teapot.

"Because many of Scott's objects pertain to things and places associated with untimely and often horrible deaths, it's less likely that a spirit would be attached to them," Victoria explained. "If you were a ghost and could go anywhere you wanted, would you choose to hang around somewhere or something with bad memories attached? There is a charged psychic energy embedded into everything that was around these items," she continued, "but like I said before, it's not spiritual energy on these."

Sometimes, though, if the object is possessed by a ghost, the distress experienced by the person coming into contact with it or wearing it is even more prominent due to the associated black energy of the ghost, although that didn't seem to be the case here. But because Victoria did sense several entities in the apartment, it was decided that we go into the living room and conduct an informal séance to see who they might be and find out why they were hanging around.

The participants that evening were Barry, Victoria, Scott, and myself along with Scott's friends Brian Eilander and Scott Woosley.

After the initial opening prayer and the placing of a protective white light around us all, Victoria thought it would be interesting to use a Ouija board to try and make contact with those who were milling about.

The use of a Ouija board is controversial, and many believe the board invites only negative entities. Some users believe that paranormal or supernatural forces are at work in spelling out Ouija board answers, while skeptics believe that those using the board either consciously or unconsciously move the pointer to what is selected. Whether one is a believer or a skeptic, it is highly recommended that the board not be used by people who "just want to have some fun" because the consequences can sometimes be quite dangerous, but if a qualified medium is conducting the séance and calls on the gatekeepers to not let any negative entities through, a supervised Ouija session can be quite interesting.

Unfortunately, our Ouija session was fairly uneventful, even though Victoria told us that there were two or three spirits in the room with us the whole time. It seems that they were more curious about what we were doing than willing to take part. When the planchette did move, it was rather sluggish, and painfully slow in spelling out several unintelligible words.

The letters *H-O-J-R-X-M-N*-and *K* were spelled out, followed by *M-N*. Very few vowels. When we asked if the spirit if it was willing to spell out its name, the planchette immediately moved to the "No" position.

Scott then asked if the person trying to communicate with us used to live in the house and Victoria asked if the spirit knew where it was. Again, the answer to both questions was "No."

While the *board* was not "talking," several of the séance participants were experiencing phenomenon. We heard several loud raps, Scott's friend, Scott W., kept breaking out in chills, and at one point, our host had the hair stand up on the back of his neck.

I had brought along a new device to try, a K2 meter that is sometimes referred to as an electronic Ouija board because the spirit can respond to questions by coming close to the device's electromagnetic sensors and lighting up a series of lights in response to questions asked.

Since this was the first time I'd tried to use the meter, Barry took it and walked throughout the house as a sort of "control situation" to see if it would go off near electrical appliances and such. He went through each room by himself while the rest of us were sitting in the living room with the Ouija board, and when he came back, he said that the meter had not responded at all. As he got closer to where we were sitting though, the lights started to flash. At first, we thought that perhaps it was responding to the camera we had set up to film the séance, but when he held the meter right up to the camera, the lights did not respond. We also looked to see that there were no other electrical outlets or appliances that would cause the meter to flash, and there weren't.

In theory, the meter is supposed to respond to *yes* and *no* questions, but this night we didn't find that to be true. What did happen, though, is that it seemed to respond to our conversation, as if expressing an opinion.

At one point, Victoria mentioned that there was a woman spirit in attendance and thought that she might be the spirit who was making noise in the living room closet, which we all clearly heard. The lights on the K2 meter began flashing wildly, as if it were giving us confirmation.

There were a total of three spirits in the room that Victoria picked up on. The first was a man named Edward, the second was a "Troll-like" spirit who was quite shy and kind of hiding out in the far corner of the room, and the third seemed to be the spirit of silent movie actress Natacha Rambova, who was the second wife of Rudolph Valentino.

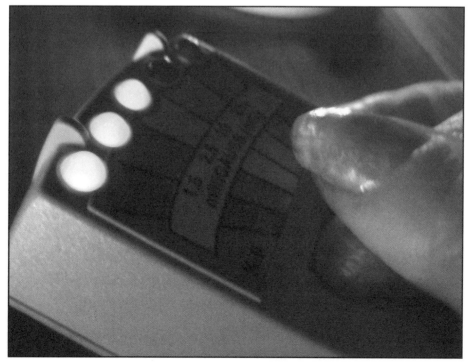

The K2 meter talking back.

We came to that conclusion primarily because of the description Victoria gave of the spirit. When she began describing the apparition, it sounded just like Rambova. Scott then went to his computer and looked in his files for a picture of the actress, and she was just as Victoria described.

Rambova and Valentino had lived together in a bungalow on Sunset Boulevard near Highland Avenue and Scott had some tiles that were once part of the bungalow's floor. Victoria thought that that particular item, and perhaps the happy time they had together, was why Rambova's spirit might be attached to that artifact.

At first we attributed the weird letters the Ouija board was putting out to the fact that maybe the spirit who was trying to communicate with us did not have a great command of the English language and thinking that

Scott pulling Natacha Rambova's picture on the computer to show Victoria.

Rambova was Russian, we came to the conclusion that it might have been her. But the actress was, in fact, not Russian, as many people believe. She was born Winifred Shaughnessy in Utah, educated abroad and changed her name when she joined a ballet troupe in Russia.

She met Rudolph Valentino when he was working on the film *Camille* in 1921. At the time, he was relatively unknown. *The Four Horsemen of the Apocalypse*, made the same year, was the hit that propelled him into stardom. Soon, the shy Valentino began wooing Rambova and they eloped on May 22nd, 1922. This event was to produce a scandal, as it was revealed that Valentino was not legally divorced from his former wife, Jean Acker. After being charged and fined for bigamy, the couple quietly re-married the following year.

After their marriage, rumors surfaced that theirs was a 'lavender marriage'—a union of convenience between two homosexuals, but it wasn't the rumors that spoiled this love affair. It seemingly was the strain of Valentino's lack of independence from his headstrong wife that led to the end of their marriage in 1926.

On her breakup with Valentino, Rambova was quoted as saying, "With butlers, maids and the rest, what work is therefor a housewife? I won't be a parasite. I won't sit home and twiddle my fingers, waiting for a husband who goes on the lot at five a.m. and gets home at midnight and receives mail from girls in Oshkosh and Kalamazoo."

When Victoria asked if it was the female spirit who inhabited the closet and if she was in fact Natacha Rambova, the K2 meter went crazy while at the same time, the Ouija board kept spelling out unintelligible words.

Brian then asked if we could perhaps try and contact his aunt, who suffered an untimely death as the result of murder four years earlier.

The Ouija board was again quite sluggish and Victoria sensed that the woman's spirit was quite weak and that the poor soul was still recuperating from her last ordeal here on Earth.

"This is quite normal for those experiencing an untimely passing," she explained, "especially with a murder." She then went on to say that spirits that pass violently or difficultly enter a hospital-like setting to regain their strength.

"I see her recuperating," she told Brian, "I see her at peace and she is with her loved ones in spirit."

Then Victoria noticed another spirit standing in the doorway to the adjacent room who said his name was Charlie. "He's tall, with black hair, distinguished looking, and he's wearing a white shirt. I think he's come over from the studio, but he's not harmful in any way. He's just observing."

At that moment, I saw a white shadow fly past Scott W.'s shoulder, and Victoria said she was feeling suddenly dizzy. There was also a definite cold spot in the space between where Victoria and I were sitting.

"Somebody keeps walking back and forth in that other room," said Victoria, pointing towards the entryway, so Barry got up and took the K2 meter to see if he could pick anything up in there. Again, the meter gave no response until he came back to our circle, and it once again lit up like a Christmas tree.

At that point, since the Ouija board was really not responding, we decided to stop trying and were just sitting around talking when Victoria turned to the living room closet. She sensed that the shy, troll-like guy we'd seen earlier had gone in there, and when we asked for confirmation by having the entity spike the meter, it again began to flash wildly. Unfortunately, we were never able to find out who this enigmatic little man was.

It was time to close the circle by then, so Victoria gave a closing prayer and we all got up to stretch our legs. Scott was still worried about us leaving unwanted spirits behind and a little bit unnerved at the thought of a strange little man in his closet, so Victoria offered to do a Banishing Pentagram to make him leave, which in essence makes the entity aware that he's not wanted and sends him on his way.

In the end, although we weren't really able to communicate clearly with the spirits in the apartment and get more information about who they were and why they were still there, Scott was pleased to find out that his keepsakes were not possessed; and since that was the real reason we were there, I'd have to say that our séance was a complete success.

When I called Scott the next day to see if he was feeling better about sharing his space with a few benign spirits, he said, "I never believed in ghosts until I moved into this apartment, but having this event in my home really left me feeling more at ease with my surroundings. I often feel like I may be crossing a line with some of the items I've "liberated" and keep in my home. Hearing from some of the individuals that they are "okay" with it, was a good thing for me."

David Wells at "The House That Fear Built"

"Each soul enters with a mission. We all have a mission to perform."

—Edgar Cayce

Courtesy Winchester Mystery House, San Jose, California.

Many people believe that communicating with the dead is not only possible, but sometimes even necessary as was the case of Sarah Winchester, the heiress of the Winchester Rifle fortune. This is one lady who was most definitely on a mission.

While the haunted Winchester House might be far from Hollywood in distance, Sarah Winchester's story is so unique, it could have easily have been concocted by

Hollywood screenwriters. Over the years, Hollywood has told Sarah's story over and over again beginning in the 1950s when the house became well known throughout the United States due to several presentations on the television show *You Asked For It*. Since then, the mass media has paid homage to the house and every psychic worth his salt has been there for an investigation

The lady of the house, Sarah Winchester, was born Sarah Lockwood Pardee in 1839. In 1862, Sarah married William Wirt Winchester, who was the son of Oliver Winchester, the famed gun manufacturer. William was heir to his father's considerable fortune valued in the millions of dollars in the early 1860s.

The Winchester family hosted William and Sarah's wedding which was held in New Haven, Connecticut, and it was quite an elaborate affair. Upon marrying William, Sarah became the belle of New Haven, and was on top of the city's social scene.

Their union went well, and in July 1866, Sarah and William had a daughter who they named Annie, but tragedy struck when Annie was only six months old. The infant died of what is now known as Crib Death. This began what Sarah believed to be a curse on her family, and she was so traumatized over her daughter's death, she nearly slipped into madness.

William and Sarah had no other children, and eventually they tried to maintain a normal life, but soon Sarah would meet with another tragedy. In March 1881, William was struck down with tuberculosis and died.

After the death of her husband, Sarah inherited more than $20 million as well as nearly 50 percent ownership of the Winchester Repeating Arms Company which brought her an income of approximately $1,000 per day, none of which was taxable until 1913. That amount was roughly equivalent to $21,000 a day in 2006 dollars.

Despite her great wealth, Sarah fell into a severe depression. She went to see a Spiritualist medium who conducted a séance. "Your husband is here," said the medium, who then went on to provide a description of William Winchester. "He says for me to tell you that there is a curse on your family, which has already taken the life of he and your child. It will soon take you too. It is a curse that has resulted from the terrible weapon created by the Winchester family. Thousands of persons have died because of it and their spirits are now seeking vengeance."

The Winchester Rifle, a total revolution in gun design became known as the "rifle that won the West." With the beginning of the Civil War on the horizon, the Winchester Repeating Arms Company began to produce thousands of rifles and obtained a fortune from government contracts.

The medium reportedly told Sarah that she had to leave her home in New Haven and travel West, where she must "build a home for yourself and for the spirits who have fallen from this terrible weapon, too. You can never stop building the house. If you continue building, you will live. Stop and you will die."

Sarah, believing that she was guided by the hand of her dead husband, traveled to California's Santa Clara Valley in 1884. Here, she found a six-room farmhouse under construction which belonged to a Dr. Caldwell. She entered into negotiations with him and soon convinced him to sell her the house and the 162 acres on which it rested.

Construction on the Mansion began in 1884 and continued twenty-our hours a day, seven days a week until the widow's death, thirty-eight years later. By then, the home was filled with so many unexplained oddities, that it came to be known as the Winchester Mystery House.

The House contained 160 rooms in all, including 40 bedrooms, 13 bathrooms, many of which have glass doors, and 6 kitchens. There are 2,000 doors in the house and 10,000 windows. One room has a window in the floor; others have closets that open to blank walls. There are many rooms within rooms and one door that opens to an eight-foot drop overlooking a garden outside. Another door opens to an eight-foot drop into a kitchen sink.

One of the first rooms that Sarah built was a Séance Room. Every night at midnight, the bells in the bell tower would ring to summon the spirits to the séance. When the séance was completed, usually around two o'clock in the morning, the bells would toll to signal that it was time for the spirits to depart. During these nightly séances, the spirits who Sarah contacted gave her explicit instructions on which additions should be made to the house. To the original eight rooms, hundreds more were added—many of them quickly ripped out to make way for the new ideas from Mrs. Winchester's nocturnal advisors. Literally miles of winding, twisting, bewildering corridors snake their way through the house, while numerous secret passageways are concealed in the walls. Some end in closets, others in blank walls. Some ceilings are so low that an average size person must stoop to avoid bumping his or her head. The explanation for all this is that the house was designed by ghosts for ghosts. If ghost stories are to be believed, spirits dearly love to vanish up chimneys so they were obligingly provided with not one but forty-seven of these escape hatches.

On September 4, 1922, after a conference session with the spirits in the séance room, Sarah went to her bedroom for the night. At some point in the early morning hours, she died in her sleep at the age of eighty-three. In the years since Sarah's death, many séances have been held at the Winchester House and the participants are rarely disappointed. Sarah is said to make frequent appearances to unwary guests as does the spirit of a man in overalls, no doubt a devoted workman. The ghosts of two servants, a man and a woman, still linger around a corner of their ex-mistress's bedroom. Employees and visitors alike tell stories of footsteps, banging noises like windows that bang so hard they shatter in the aftermath, apparitions, mysterious voices from beyond, organ music playing, and book pages turning by unseen hands.

When Chris Fleming investigated the Winchester House for an episode of *Dead Famous* in 2004, he experienced quite a bit of activity, but he says he can't remember much of the investigation after the séance which he considered to be successful, but also a disaster. Unfortunately, he says, he didn't ground himself properly and lost control after being flooded by spirits. He felt as if he was suffocating and could not get them off of him. Watching the events play out on television was quite frightening. According to Chris, "The Séance room is an incredible doorway for communicating with other side. "

It's interesting to note that when the TAPS team from *Ghost Hunters* visited the Winchester House, although they had a couple of personal experiences, they didn't come up with any hard evidence at all that the house was haunted.

David Wells and the *Most Haunted* team conducted a seven-hour live investigation in November 2007, and their findings, for the most part, were similar to those of Jason, Grant, and the TAPS team.

"The energy in the house is quite odd," David told me a couple of weeks after their investigation, "but to be honest with you, I think the house was quite disappointing. There was an energy moving around and shifting in the house but it was not as active as some people claim it is. The spirits are there, and it does sometimes feel as though you are being followed, but I also feel that because it is a tourist attraction and is heavily fished as far as paranormal investigations go, the spirits are bored. They've seen it all before and don't pay a lot of attention. I think that before it is ever investigated again, it needs to be shut down for a couple of years to give them all a rest. There is most definitely something inside the Winchester House, but it's worn out, I suspect."

"It was a house of stereotypes," he continued, referring to the array of colorful spirits he was picking up. "There was a Red Indian, a lay preacher, and a little girl. I was thinking, 'Is this *Scary Movie 2*, or what?' When I first walked in, we did a walk around so we knew where we were going, and with all these caricature-like spirits, it was like, 'Where's the rest of the Village People?'

"I was unnerved a couple of times during our investigation," he admits. "The first occurrence was with one of our team members, Cath. She is very sensitive, and I think she's becoming more so, and what happened to her during our investigation was the most remarkable event of the evening. Because you're working with such powerful stuff, it's sometimes really hard to keep the spirits off, and during one of our séances that night, there was a spirit who tried to communicate with us but couldn't, so it shot right across the table to Cath.

"I think the most interesting thing about that was that she looked down and saw that her hands were not her hands and the experience played havoc with her emotions for the rest of the night."

Even Dr. Ciarán O'Keeffe, the show's usually skeptical parapsychologist, claims to have been "flummoxed" at some of the activity that went on. David said that while he doesn't recall when or in what context Ciarán said that, he knows that the parapsychologist was greatly concerned about what happened to Cath.

"Ciarán was also initially confused about the EVP we picked up, but eventually we found that it was a crew member's voice in the background. When you're in the midst of it, you don't hear everything. Also, people forget that EVP isn't the voice of someone or something you would hear. It's something you would hear on the tape but not something that would be recorded on the machine. They change it *in* the machine, not *off* the machine, if that makes sense."

"I was also kind of freaked when they brought in one of the Winchester rifles because any kind of killing thing is hideous to touch, isn't it? But while I was horrified by the gun, the house itself didn't scare me to death. It was kind of like a Disney house of horrors. If a skeleton had dropped down from the ceiling and its eyes were glowing green, I wouldn't have been surprised."

David did come in contact with the spirit of Sarah Winchester, but as he tells it,

"I was wondering what to do next because she completely ignored me. Turned her back to me. She was very much going about her own business and while I wanted to step in her face and say 'Hello!', since it was her house, I decided to be more respectful."

One entity that did pay attention to David was the lay preacher, who found it amusing to play around with David's face.

"He took control of my mouth and I couldn't speak properly for a while, and then during the séance we conducted in the Séance room, he poked my eyes a couple of times, but while that was uncomfortable, at the same time he made me laugh because he reminded me so much of Colonel Sanders.

"There's something odd about the Séance Room itself," admits David, "and I'm not convinced that they've got the right room, although it did feel as though it was the vibrating center of the building. And there's also something odd about the fact that no one would have a séance every night for thirty-eight years and not become more advanced, because you couldn't stop yourself, you

Sarah Winchester.

couldn't do that for two hours every single night and then just pop off to bed. That couldn't have happened. Sarah would have wanted more.

"The other strange thing was that there were no books in the entire house that belonged to her and they don't know what her library consisted of. Books are the pathway of how we know people and they don't know anything about her. Nothing in the house belonged to her. Nothing, not one thing. It's all too clean. It's almost as though there's been a clean-up crew put in and it's all gone.

"Sarah's essence is around there and I did spot her a couple of times, fleetingly, but then you have to ask yourself why she would want to stay there? I think she just comes back when she thinks there's something interesting going on and is not there all the time. I guess a TV crew there would be interesting to her, but I really don't think that she's there very often.

"There is a caretaker ghost and the Indian who seem to be the ones who are there more permanently. The Preacher was probably not the type of person that Sarah would have had in her house when she was alive. That's the argument I got from Ciaran and some of the guys, but Sarah opened up the doorway with her séances and who knows who the Hell is coming through? If he was flying around the place during one of her séances, he would have been quite happy to stay there, thank you very much."

During the séance itself, the table moved, the temperature in the room dropped quite a bit, and aside from being poked in the eye, and at one point feeling as though he was going to be sick, David had hoped for a bit more—considering that the energy in the room would have been built up over all those years.

"On a personal level, I had hoped to physically see something even if no one else got to see it, because I thought the energy would be strong enough to do that. So there was a big disappointment that that didn't happen.

"I also wanted to get under Sarah Winchester's skin because I was intrigued by the whole séance room, and the '*robeing up* thing' she did. There's something odd about her *robeing up*. That's not Spiritualist. Spiritualists don't robe. That's more Cultist, and I wanted to find out what her beliefs really were, whether Pagan, Kabala, what was her Diety—but she wasn't giving anything away.

"I think I said it that night, but let Sarah's experience with mediums be a lesson to us all. Sarah was told that she would die if she didn't build this house. Who is a medium to tell anyone that? Here was a woman who was pampered within an inch of her life and who was searching for purpose and reason, and a medium tells her to keep building or she would die. Well, hello, Luv, you're going to die sometime. I would have been the first to say, 'Oh, get a grip of yourself and use your money for better things.'

"The intensity of her emotion and who she was, and how she thought things had to be built remains in the house," says David. But since Sarah chose to remain an enigma, he summed up his experience at The Winchester Mystery house by saying, "It's a house with secrets that will never be uncovered."

Hans Holzer's Hollywood Ghosts

"Celebrity ghosts are no different from the ghosts of the unknown, but the interest in them, naturally, is at least as great as the fascination with the celebrity involved."

—Hans Holzer

Professor Hans Holzer, world renowned ghost hunter and author of well over 100 books on the subject of ghosts and hauntings is a leading authority in the field of the paranormal.

I might have mentioned this before, but when I was growing up, Hans Holzer was my favorite author. While all the other kids in my elementary school would go to the library and check out *The Cat in the Hat* and *Nancy Drew*, I could be found in the adult paranormal section picking out *Ghost Hunter* books. He was my idol.

Holzer once said,

"We all pass out of the physical body and we are now on the other side of life. It's a world just like this one—it has only two differences: there's no sense of time, and if you're ill when you die, you're now no longer ill. But other than that, you'll find houses, trees, gardens, and your relatives, friends, and so on. It looks like a very real world. Maybe a little nicer, but still a normal, real world. And you are just the way you were before. Maybe a little bit younger-looking if you wish, but you're still in a very real world.

"Spirits are people who have left the physical body but are very much alive in a thinner, etheric body with which they are able to function pretty much the same way they did in the physical body, although they are no longer weighted down by physical objects, distances, time, and space. The majority of those who die become free spirits, though a tiny fraction are unable to proceed into the next stage and must remain behind because of emotional difficulties."

He also added that those who have gone on are not necessarily gone forever and are anxious to keep a hand in situations they left on the Earth plane. He tells us that life is a bureaucracy on the other side as it is here amongst the living.

"You can't just call Uncle Frank (who's still living)," he explained. "You have to get permission from a group of people who call themselves guides—spirit guides. They will say, 'Why do you want to make contact? What's your purpose?' And if they approve of it, they'll say, 'Okay, find yourself a medium somewhere, speak with them, and they will make contact for you.' Or if you're that strong, you can try to make contact yourself.

When asked if he is ever fearful during investigations, Holzer replied,

"There's nothing out there that isn't one way or the other human. Hollywood notwithstanding, there are no monsters out there. There is no other supernatural race, no devils, no fellows in red underwear. It doesn't exist."

Over the years, Hollywood has played a part in many of Dr. Holzer's investigations and he has been up close and personal with a number of Hollywood ghosts.

"On the famed dead," says Holzer, "it doesn't matter who they were on earth as when we pass, we are very similar. Many have reported over the years of haunted celebrity sightings, where they are the same as any other ghost. They are unable to cross over and have unfinished business. They are there trying to make contact to receive help. That's when you get a well trained transmedium and parapsychologist to investigate, famous or not. The interest in celebrity ghosts is at least as great as the fascination with the celebrity involved and offers a unique perspective for anyone curious about what happens to the rich and famous in the next world."

Elvis Presley

One of Dr. Holzer's most fascinating conversations was with the spirit of Elvis Presley. He has made contact with The King several times since the singer's untimely passing in 1977, and says that Elvis is more "alive" today than ever.

"I wrote a book on Elvis Presley," said Dr. Holzer recently, "because I met a woman who said she had met him during astral projection travel. Elvis had told her he knew her in another life and wanted to connect to her. Through a transmedium, this information came through and so I documented it."

That session was held on July 13, 1978, nearly a year after Presley left the physical world. During the session, Elvis said that he was worried about his father's health and probably for good reason because Vernon died of heart failure not long afterwards.

"Elvis also said that he believed in the power of psychic healing and that he himself had the ability to heal while he was here on Earth but didn't have enough time to follow through with it," said Holzer. He also wanted to let people know that the spirit world really does exist, and was very upset about the book written about him by people he once considered to be close friends.

"They made me sound like I should be in a home, that I was crazy," said Elvis, referring to the book, *Elvis What Happened?* by Red West, Sonny Hebler, and Dave West that came out in 1977. Written by three of his closest companions, the tome tells a shocking and unflattering story which really upset Elvis. "They wrote lies, they blew it up, turned on me. They hurt me; they hurt me. I trusted them. I trusted them with my life."

During a subsequent séance conducted by Dr. Holzer in 1998, The King talked about his family, his friends, the fact that he felt as though no American had ever been more exploited than he had been. Then he went on to discuss his life as an entertainer, both during his lifetime and on the Other Side.

"I was born in your world and reborn in spirit to entertain, and I make a little bit of music with a few close friends like Roy Orbison and Buddy Holly. The shows I do over here are bigger and better and are like big spirituals—gatherings if you like. You know, that's always something I wanted to do in the body but the Colonel never really let me get the chance to do it. Money, money, money, that's all he ever wanted. Still, I suppose that was his job and he must have loved it, the old son of a b----! In his thinking, he's still my manager here, you know! Well, it's all about being personally happy over here and it sure seems to make him happy."

When asked what his conditions are in the afterlife, Elvis said,

"Things are whatever we want them to be over here. We go to school and everybody has a job to do. I'm doing a lot of work to inspire people, to help others live better lives on the Earth plane."

When Elvis was alive, he was once quoted as saying, "Truth is like the sun. You can shut it out for a time, but it ain't goin' away."   That belief still holds true when he expressed his feelings about people's skepticism about life after death. He told Holzer to pass on the message that he is still here, he is whole, he is well, and also wants people to believe that their loved ones still exist in the afterlife, that they are well, and that they want to communicate with their loved ones. He said that people should believe in reincarnation and if they did, "it would change the world and mankind wouldn't be so damn stupid."

Clifton Webb

Several years ago, Dr. Holzer was called out to investigate the former home of the late actor Clifton Webb, probably best know as the classy villain, Waldo Lydecker, in *Laura* (1944), and as Elliott Templeton in *The Razor's Edge* (1946), both of which won him Oscar nominations. It is said, however, that his portrayal of the priggish *Mr. Belvedere* was supposedly not far removed from his real life persona. What might be less known but equally interesting about the actor is that it was Clifton Webb who first introduced Irving Berlin's classic song "Easter Parade" on the Broadway stage, and it is acknowledged that Mr. Webb was the inspiration for the persnickety Mr. Peabody in the cartoon series, *The Adventures Rocky and Bullwinkle*.

It was during Dr. Holzer's investigation of Clifton Webb's residence that he and psychic medium Sybil Leek ran into probably one of the most cantankerous spirits they'd ever met.

Clifton Webb passed away in from a heart attack in 1966 at the age of seventy-two, but after having lived in his beloved home for over twenty years, his spirit remained, much to the chagrin of the new tenants. From the day they moved into the house, strange things began to happen.

On moving day, the married couple and the man's mother were standing near the pool in the courtyard and looking towards the house when they saw a ghostly figure swaying in the distance. The following morning, the mother woke up to find her cigarettes broken in half, the pack crushed, and tobacco strewn all over her bed. (Webb had been an avid non-smoker during the final years of his life.) The couple's dogs and cats began acting strangely and would avoid certain areas of the house, many apparitions were seen, and the servants often complained of lights going off and on by themselves, toilet paper rolls unrolled on their own, and the maid claimed to have been attacked by a cold presence. A year to the day that Webb died, the owners woke up to the sound of moaning in their bedroom and a gray figure forming in the corner of the room.

A real estate agent approached the couple shortly thereafter with an offer to buy the property. While they had no intention of selling, they jokingly quoted a ridiculously-high asking price which, to their surprise, was accepted, but after looking around and finding that home prices in the area had risen dramatically, they decided to stay put. That night, the lady of the house woke up in the wee hours of the morning to rustling sounds in the bedroom and heard a voice saying, "Well, well, well, " which was a phrase that Clifton Webb uttered quite often.

Wanting to find out perhaps how they could appease Webb's restless spirit, the couple invited Dr. Holzer out to investigate.

After assembling themselves in the Greek Room, Webb's favorite room in the house, they called out and offered the medium as in instrument of communication in which any willing spirits could use to come through.

A spirit came though immediately, first asking for a drink and then expressing an urge to sing. When Holzer asked the entity what sort of song he'd like to sing, the sardonic response was, "Dead men tell no tales." Holzer then tried to coax the entity into revealing his name. At first, the reply was, "Webb of intrigue," but shortly there after came "Webb, Webb, W-E-B-B," and his true identity was made.

Throughout the rest of the séance, Mr. Webb's ghost complained of being lonely, wanted to be heard, angrily talked about people he didn't care for during his lifetime, and, claiming to hate all newspapermen, distrustfully accused Holzer of being one himself. When asked why he remained in the house, the late actor's answer was, "I like it and I have a right to be here."

At one point, the discussion became quite emotional and the entity cried out, "Damn you, leave me alone." As the sobbing got heavier, Holzer decided it was best to release the entity and allow him to go in peace.

Friends of Webb who were at the séance and knew him well confirmed the identity of the people Webb's ghost talked about, his negative reaction to having a "newspaperman" present, and verified that the mannerisms and phrases manifesting from Sybil Leek during the séance were very much in the style of Clifton Webb.

For a short while after the séance, it appeared that Clifton Webb had his say and the house was quiet, but the consummate actor did not stay away for long and continues to haunt his beloved Beverly Hills home to this day.

Growing Up Haunted

Hans Holzer's daughter, Alexandra grew up believing in the afterlife and speaks of some of her séance experiences in her new book on the subject entitled, *Growing Up Haunted.*

Alexandra says,

"*Growing Up Haunted* has become this author's catch phrase, or so it seems. At first, I was rather leery in going with it as I was not sure what readers would think of it or me. New to the paranormal field and also the publishing industry, I was simply trying to break ground. Many have come to me in awe of my father who in turn had pioneered the ghost business taking it to a new level in the sixties. When Eileen Garret and her Foundation sought out my father, it was not only a chance to further his ventures into the unknown, but also an opportunity to pave the path for many today in the paranormal."

I asked Alexandra what it was like growing up in a "ghosite" environment. "It was very normal, as that is what we knew," she said. "For us, normal would seem abnormal."

Séances were commonplace in the Holzer household for many years.

"I recall a time ... from stories from my parents. I wasn't around for many of them as they stopped a bit after I came along, but as a child, I would off and on see white figures, distorted out of the corner of my eye while watching TV in the living room. I also felt like I was being watched, and not just in our NY home. When I was with my Parisian grandmother out in Eastern Long Island, it felt like I was never alone. Going to bed at night was very difficult for me at times throughout my life."

To read more about Alexandra's experiences, *Growing Up Haunted*, visit her web site at www.HauntingHolzer.com.

Richard Senate Talks to Old Hollywood Ghosts

Dying is a very dull, dreary affair. And my advice to you is to have nothing whatever to do with it.

—W. Somerset Maugham

R ichard Senate is one of the most prominent ghost investigators of our time. He has written many books on the subject of ghosts and paranormal phenomenon, as well as having appeared on a multitude of television and radio shows dealing with the subject. He's also a well respected lecturer on the topic.

While not all of Richard's encounters have been with Hollywood ghosts, a great many have been, and the following story puts a new spin on the untimely death of silent screen star Rudolph Valentino. In fact, Valentino himself claims to have been murdered.

It is commonly believed that after completing work on the film *The Son of the Sheik*, Valentino went on a nationwide tour to promote the film. On August 15, 1926, the actor collapsed in pain at the Hotel Ambassador in New York City. He was hospitalized at the Polyclinic in New York and underwent surgery for a perforated ulcer. The surgery went well and he seemed to be recovering when peritonitis set in and spread throughout his body. He died eight days later, at the age of thirty-one.

When his death was announced, American women became hysterical. Some even committed suicide. Rioting broke out in the crowds who were waiting to see his open coffin at his public viewing (though they didn't know that his body had been replaced by a wax dummy—a second casket in a back room contained his real body).

Given his reputation as a ladies man, rumors immediately begin to circulate that Valentino had died at the hand of a jilted lover or a jealous husband. After all, Valentino was a man of great passion. He was married twice, the first time to actress Jean Acker and the second go-round with to Natacha Rambova, but he dated many beautiful women (and a few men?) in his time, so it's no wonder people believed he died that way.

Another rumor about Valentino's untimely death came to pass when his last paramour, Pola Negri, stated in her autobiography that Valentino was concerned about a receding hairline and was taking a drug—probably illegal—to stop his hair loss. Could the drug have precipitated his death at such a young age?

In time, the rumors eventually died down, but it seems that Valentino himself wanted to set the record straight once and for all, so at a séance conducted by Richard Senate on March 17, 1990, "The Sheik" came through and had a great deal to say.

"The house where the séance took place stands not far from the beach in the Oxnard Silver Strand area in California," says Senate. "The house is old, one of the oldest in the area. The cottage was built for, or perhaps rented by, Paramount Studios in 1920 when a classic silent film was made on the sand dunes here. The film was titled *The Sheik* and would become the vehicle that would launch a young dancer, Rudolph Valentino, into international super-stardom. The beach cottage is also rumored to be haunted. An investigation of the house confirmed that two restless ghosts wandered there. One would identify itself as that of the silent actor himself!

"This is part of the séance transcribed from one of the visits. If the stories are true, it may well open a new criminal case into the log of unsolved mysteries of old Hollywood, a log that is full to overflowing now.

"The medium was holding a piece of costume jewelry worn by Valentino in the making of the film *The Son of The Sheik,* his last picture before his tragic death. This item was used to focus her psychic gifts in the attempt to communicate with the silent actor.

Richard: Is anyone there?
Medium: What?
Richard: Who is this; who has joined our circle tonight?
Medium: *(Smiles)* Don't you know me?
Richard: No, should we know you?
Medium: I am famous, at least I was.
Richard: Are you a film star?
Medium: Are you a fanatic?
Richard: Did you once live here?
Medium: I lived many places; I still live many places.
Richard: Are you Rudolph Valentino?
Medium: Oui.
Richard: You were the Sheik in the movies?
Medium: Yes, I played the Sheik in the moving pictures, but I played many parts in my life. Sometimes I was the lover, sometimes the fool. More times the fool I suspect.
Richard: What do you mean?

Medium: My wife, I was her fool—her plaything. She was with me at the production. We spent many happy hours here in this house. It was our love house. You can hear the sea at night.

Richard: You mean she stayed with you here during the filming of *The Sheik*?

Medium: That's what I said. The studios didn't want to have her around but she came at night and we danced in the nude, in the moonlight….(*censored*)

Richard: Why are you here?

Medium: I wait for her to comeback. I walk the balcony in the moonlight.

Richard: Didn't she divorce you?

Medium: I am a Roman Catholic—there is no divorce, never. I loved her.

Richard: Didn't she leave the United States?

Medium: She will return. Our love is greater than the bonds of this life.

Richard: Didn't you see other women?

Medium: What can I say? I am Italian. A man has needs.

Richard: Do you have a message for us tonight?

Medium: Yes, I want my fans to know that I forgive he who murdered me.

Richard: Murder? Your death was natural causes.

Medium: You, my friend, must not always believe what the newspapers say.

Richard: Doctors said it was a rupture in your stomach— some always thought it was poison.

Medium: Doctors can be made to say many things. I now know it was poison.

Richard: Who? Why?

Medium: Love, is a terrible thing sometimes.

Richard: Did your wife poison you?

Medium: No. It was another. He was the most powerful man in the United States. He could kill, and did kill, but was never suspected.

Richard: Who?

Medium: A man who bent the rules. I thought I was his friend. I went to his ranch and ate at his table. We were as brothers but hate, jealousy, changed him into an unknown enemy.

Richard: His name, give us his name.

Medium: William Randolph Hearst.

Richard: You mean the Hearst Castile man? The newspaper giant?

Medium: He suspected that I and his mistress, Marion Davis, were lovers. He was correct in that we shared our passion, but we were friends, close friends more than lovers.

Richard: You slept with Marion Davis?

Medium: That shocks you?

Richard: That would provide a motive for killing you. But you died in New York.

Medium: WR had many contacts in New York. He knew many people and many owed him favors, even those in the Black Hand.

Richard: What happened—how were you murdered?

Medium: That last night I went to a party on Park Avenue. We had gone to a Speakeasy earlier. The party was filled with women and men. There wine flowed like water. There was cocaine and brandy. Someone made me a cocktail, someone who was once rich but had lost his wealth, someone who would become rich again with the help of Hearst.

Richard: You drank it?

Medium: He was an Iscariot.

Richard: It was poison?

Medium: I do not know the name of the poison, I am not a Borgia. But I fell ill and was taken back to my hotel. I never really recovered.

Richard: Did you suspect Hearst at once?

Medium: No, I thought it was bad booze at first. It was only after the transition was I told the truth by my spirit guides. But, I hold no ill feelings, only pity.

Richard: Spirit guides?

Medium: I have two guides; an Indian from your west and an ancient Egyptian priest. They guide me still.

Richard: What do you do now?

Medium: I have projects. I plan on a moving picture *El Cid*. I will play the Cid. I help others too. They do not know I am here but I help them make photoplays.

Richard: You are still in Hollywood?

Medium: Yes, I walk the studios and stages. I go unseen into the places where dancers practice. I am there with the young directors and young men. I help them with ideas, with scenarios and, always I wait for my beloved wife.

Richard: As a Catholic, don't you expect to go to a heaven?

Medium: We will go together, hand in hand, to paradise.

Richard: Didn't you have a girlfriend when you died? Pola Negri?

Medium: We had fun together. She could dance.

Richard: Some said you two would marry?

Medium: No. But, I must say that Pola was the only woman who ever made friends with Kabar.

Richard: Who is Kabar?

Medium: My dog. The only one of my dogs I let sleep on my bed. We would be together the three of us.

Richard: Some say you were a homosexual—were you?

Medium: Don't believe those rumors. I am Italian. I love pleasure, yes, I am not perfect and there were times in Paris that things happened. You must be a man of the world to find success in Hollywood. But, I am a man who loves women. Yes, perhaps I loved them too much.

Richard: So you were not a homosexual?

Medium: I did not suffer from the English Disease.

Richard: How can we know what really happened when you were poisoned.

Medium: You must trust me. Those who knew and could prove things are now over here. They too had to die. They were taken by mysterious accidents, strange diseases, and suicides that were not. I forgive them—and I forgive WR.

Richard: Have you seen him in the afterlife?

Medium: Marion yes, others I knew and loved, but not my wife, and not WR.

Richard: Do you think he went to that other place?

Medium: It is all up to God. Good night my friend, good night.

Newspaper magnate William Randolph Hearst was a powerful force to reckon with back in his day. After acquiring *The New York Journal* in the late 1800s, Hearst engaged in a bitter circulation war with Joseph Pulitzer's *New York World* that led to the creation of "yellow journalism"— sensationalized stories of dubious veracity. Acquiring more newspapers, Hearst ultimately created a chain that at its peak numbered nearly thirty papers in major American cities. Eventually, he expanded into magazines as well, building an enormous publishing empire.

Although he was elected twice to the U. S. House of Representatives, he was defeated in 1906 in a race for governor of New York. By 1925, Hearst had established or acquired newspapers in every section of the United States, as well as several magazines. He also published books of fiction and produced motion pictures featuring the actress Marion Davies, his mistress for more than thirty years.

Through his newspapers and magazines, Hearst exercised enormous political influence, most notably in whipping up the public frenzy that pushed the U. S. into war with Spain in 1898. Some regard him as the model for the leading character in Orson Welles classic film, *Citizen Kane*. It's certainly not out of the question that a cover-up of any involvement he might have had in Valentino's demise could have easily been arranged, especially given the speculation that he was also involved in the death of silent film producer Thomas Harper Ince two years before.

Officially, Ince died of a heart attack while on a weekend yacht trip to celebrate this forty-third birthday with Hearst, Davies, and other prominent Hollywood personalities. For years, rumors circulated that Hearst caught his mistress, Marion Davies, kissing Charlie Chaplin and shot at him, accidentally hitting and killing Ince instead.

The Hearst-Davies liaison endured for three and a half decades and was, unlike most other extra-marital affairs of that time, an almost-open book. The two appeared in public frequently, with her hanging onto his arm. But, in true chivalrous fashion, he tried to shield Marion from negative publicity as much as possible by simply not reporting on it. Neither did the rival publications. Hearst was just too powerful an adversary to risk antagonizing. It is said that he was steadfastly faithful to Marion, even while being unfaithful to his legal wife, Millicent, although Marion was probably unfaithful to him.

The small party on board—including Louella Parsons, who later made a deal with Hearst for a syndicated gossip column—were sworn to secrecy and Hearst used his power to cover up the murder. Patty Hearst's 1994 novel, *Murder at San Simeon*, and a fictional 2001 film, *The Cat's Meow*, are based on these rumors. Hearst was reportedly extremely jealous of Davies, who had been involved in an affair with Charlie Chaplin—one of several paramours she would have over the years. According to the stories, jealous lover Hearst went into a rage that day, mistook Ince for Chaplin, shot him accidentally and then reported that Ince died of natural causes.

So, is it possible that Valentino was the victim of another of Hearst's jealous rages? There is little to connect Davies and Valentino as a hot item, but they certainly knew each other. In her autobiography, Davis included a picture of Valentino and her dancing together in bathing suits, and Hearst's castle-like estate at San Simeon, La Cuesta Encantada ("The Enchanted Hill") was a Mecca for the Hollywood elite. And Valentino was certainly at the top of the *A List* during his heyday.

Invitations to The Castle were highly coveted during the 1920s and '30s. Guests usually flew into the estate's airfield or took a private Hearst-owned train car from Los Angeles. Charlie Chaplin, Cary Grant, the Marx Brothers, Charles Lindbergh, Joan Crawford, Calvin Coolidge, and Winston Churchill were among Hearst's A-list guests, but according to Richard Senate, "The Castle said that Valentino never visited there (or the records were pulled out by Mr. Hearst) but others say they saw him there."

It seems a bit odd that Valentino had never visited San Simeon, but then again, it's quite possible that Hearst, knowing of Davies' roving eye, merely tried to weed out his competition.

Whether or not Valentino was ever a guest at The Castle is immaterial. In the case of Valentino's untimely death, though, it's just a matter of who you are going to believe, and as my good friend Kenny Kingston always says, "Spirits don't lie."

A few years later, Richard Senate had the opportunity to talk to another of William Randolph Hearst's alleged victims. Thomas Ince. But unlike Valentino, Ince claims that his death was accidental, and not at the hands of WRH.

"This was made after a tour of the old Ince Studio in Culver City for the British TV show *Dead Famous*," said Richard. "A séance was conducted with Psychic Chris Fleming at the site and a Séance held at the famous Ship Room of the old studio—now called the Culver Studios. The place has many ghosts in its old sound stages. A ghostly actress did come though but she proved to be a silent star linked to Cecil B. DeMile (she was in *King of Kings* playing Mary Magdeline.) She was looking for DeMile.

"We held our own séance to gain information on the mysterious death of Thomas Ince on Mr. Hearst's Yacht, a mystery that has long haunted Hollywood. Once again, Debra Senate was the medium."

Debbie: Where am I?

Richard: You are in a hotel room.

Debbie: Where?

Richard: Los Angeles, California.

Debbie: I need to call someone.

Richard: Who are you?

Debbie: Don't you know me?

Richard: No, I don't know you.

Debbie: Yes, you're not Harry.

Richard: Who are you?

Debbie: Thomas Ince—the owner of the studio. You work for me.

Richard: Do you know you have passed on?

Debbie: I may have been drunk but....

Richard: You are dead.

Debbie: No. Are you crazy? You must have had some bad booze or something.

Richard: Do you remember your last day?

Debbie: What sort of Humbug is this?

Richard: You were on a yacht.

Debbie: I ...do...remember. It was WR and Marion... It was my birthday.

Richard: Yes, you joined the party late.

Debbie: That scamp Chaplin was there as well. Marion always knew how to throw a party.

Richard: Something happened didn't it?

Debbie: I became ill—it wasn't seasickness mind you.

Richard: Yes, then something else.

Debbie: I see it now. I was shot.

Richard: Did Mr. Hearst shoot you?

Debbie: I saw myself in the bunk—there was blood. Blood all over the blankets.

Richard: You were in bed?

Debbie: I was sick—I retired for the night. I heard a loud report—then darkness. Then I could look down and see myself like I was watching a movie, but it was in color. I was dead. My eyes were open but they were dead eyes. I have seen death in my life. Then I heard a scream. It was Marion and another woman.

Richard: What happened?

Debbie: It was an accident. I know it happened as an accident. Marion was playing with the pistol. She slipped and the thing went off. The bullet when through the thin walls of the yacht and struck me as I slept. It was a dumb accident. She was screaming about her life was over and she said she would throw herself over the side. Mr. Hearst comforted her as did Charlie. He said he would take care of everything.

Richard: So Marion killed you?

Debbie: It was an accident—I liked Marion, I liked her a lot, better than I liked Hearst.

Richard: Why were you on the yacht?

Debbie: I was hoping to get Hearst's help for the studio. We were losing money on our western pictures. We needed to branch out. Hearst wanted to expand his motion picture business. I figured with Marion's help we could put together a deal. It might have worked too.

Richard: Why do you walk the studio?

Debbie: Because its mine—They still make pictures there. I like to watch, sometime I help the young directors and even some of the actors.

Richard: How do you help?

Debbie: Give them ideas—I can do that—whisper in their ears and they think its their own ideas. Some of these new people are good too.

Richard: Are you working on anything new now?

Debbie: Yes, and its going to be great. Get this, a picture …. What… what do you say? I got to go now. They say I have to go.

Richard: Who says you must go?

Debbie: Good Bye—for now.

The séance ended—but who was it who terminated the séance? More questions? More mysteries.

John C. Fremont Public Library

"I don't believe in an afterlife, so I don't have to spend my whole life fearing hell, or fearing heaven even more. For whatever the tortures of hell, I think the boredom of heaven would be even worse."

—Isaac Asimov

As I mentioned earlier on, a séance can be preformed in a variety ways and doesn't necessarily have to be conducted in a formal manner with a group of people sitting around a table, hands joined. Whenever a medium is able to speak to a spirit or have the spirit channel through them, that can be considered a séance. And since there were places that I wanted to investigate that would not allow us to bring in our camera equipment and close their business while we went about ours, Victoria

Gross and I decided to venture out on our own and conduct what I call "mini séances" in several Hollywood locations. Our first stop was the John C. Fremont Public Library.

The Library's history begins in 1912, when a group of public-spirited citizens opened the Colgrove Station reading room at Vine Street and Santa Monica Boulevard in Hollywood. It was designated as a sub-branch of the Hollywood Branch Library in 1916, then the reading room moved to a bungalow in 1923 that was erected on the grounds of the Vine Street Elementary School where a young Marilyn Monroe learned her ABCs.

In 1923, voters approved a bond measure for the construction of new library branches, including a permanent home for the bungalow, which was now known as the Santa Monica Boulevard Branch Library.

The bungalow was moved to the corner of Melrose Avenue and Seward Street in 1925 in anticipation of the construction of a new permanent branch on the corner of Melrose Avenue and June Street. The Board of Library Commissioners that year also voted to change the branch's name to the John C. Fremont Branch to honor the noted American explorer, soldier, and politician. Fremont, known by the nickname "Trailblazer," played a major role in the 1846 "Bear Flag" Revolt and in the American conquest of California.

Construction of the new branch began on December 26, 1926, and was completed in May of 1927. The branch opened on June 1 with no chairs or tables for the first week. Apparently this did not deter patrons, who leaned against book shelves or just sat on the floor to read.

The building, who's architectural style has been described as early Italian with a touch of Spanish, has since earned a position on the National Register of Historic Places and has been designated a Historic Cultural Monument of the City of Los Angeles.

In 1990, the building was closed in compliance with the Los Angeles City Building and Safety Commission's earthquake hazard reduction order because the branch's masonry was unreinforced and did not meet seismic safety codes. The branch was reopened on March 26, 1996. Among the improvements to the building were the addition of a meeting room, a small parking lot, air conditioning, wiring for computer and Internet access, access for the disabled, and an outdoor courtyard.

Victoria and I decided to pop into the library one evening right before closing to see if it was indeed haunted, because when I called the library a few days before our visit and asked the librarian if she thought the library might have a resident ghost or two, she referred me to the library web site where a picture taken in the main reading room in the 1940s shows what could be considered a ghostly presence. The photo gives a view of the main reading room, but the picture is quite distorted due to what looks like a big ectoplasmic blob right in the middle. The librarian jokingly called it their "ghost photo" and said it would be fine if we came by to check the place out.

When we first walked in, I noticed the ghost photo hanging on a nearby wall and pointed it out to Victoria. She agreed that it certainly looked paranormal and after studying it for a minute or two said she felt as though it was a woman's energy that the camera had picked up.

After a quick and quiet walk around, Victoria felt as though there was more than one ghost present and was drawn to the adult fiction section which is part of the new construction.

As we walked down one of the aisles, a reference book on Hollywood, which was standing up alone on one of the shelves suddenly toppled itself over and flew off the shelf. I caught it just before it landed on the floor. An omen perhaps?

"There's the spirit of a man standing right over there," said Victoria, pointing to the far corner of the room. He's not shy about making his presence known and is very communicative. He roams the whole library and I think he makes books drop from time to time. He's probably the one that made that Hollywood book fly off the shelf. Victoria continued,

"I see him as about fifty years old, very distinguished and I think he's British. He's very prim and proper and he's giving me the name Andrew or Sir Andrew. He's not connected with the library per se, but he watches the children who come into the library in a protective manner. But I also think he's been known to give kids a gentle smack on the head when they misbehave in here.

"I don't think he believed in an afterlife and that's the reason he hasn't crossed over, but he's fine as he is.

At that point I walked over to the reference desk and asked if there had once been a house where this new section of the library was built and the librarian said there had been, so perhaps the distinguished gentleman once lived in the area that he now haunts.

Victoria also picked up the spirit of a woman in the same section. Could it perhaps be Sir Andrew's wife?

Additionally, there was a strong female presence in the back of the library towards the head librarian's office. Victoria picked up the name Agnes and felt that she might have worked in the library, perhaps as a librarian, in the 1920s.

I was able to contact the research center of the library the next day and they checked the complete list of staff members from the 1920s and 30s, and while there was an Ann listed, there was no Agnes. It was their suggestion that perhaps Agnes was merely a dedicated patron.

When we walked outside into the courtyard Victoria picked up on another male energy.

"While the man inside is from the 20s or 30s, this man goes back even farther. This is more "rancho" style here because I see horses and buggies. I would say this is from around the 1800s. There's a very strong feeling of that. Mexican cowboys, a working ranch."

Library parking lot and courtyard.

Because Victoria didn't know we were going to the library, she had no way of knowing anything about the property which was indeed a working ranch at one time. The library is located in the Hancock Park area of Hollywood and was once part of a huge parcel of land called Rancho LaBrea. On November 16, 1860, Jose Jorge Rocha, the son of Don Antonio Jose Rocha, deeded Rancho La Brea to Major Henry Hancock and his brother John Hancock who had selected the old Spanish grant consisting of about 4,000 acres as a homestead, and for many years devoted the property to the raising of sheep and cattle.

"Something strong must have happened in this area," said Victoria, "because there is quite a bit of residual energy here. This is where I see people working horses, taming them, and the energy is very strong. But at the same time, there is a young girl here as well. I feel like she was raped and murdered in this area sometime in the 1800s. This spirit doesn't go into the library, she's not part of that, but she is appearing to me in two different ways. Once when she was very young, I would say fourteen or fifteen years old, and again in her early twenties. I'd say she died violently when she was twenty-one, but was the victim of sexual abuse for several years before she passed.

"I think she was a worker on the ranch, and it wouldn't surprise me if the house that once stood here or even the house next door is haunted. There's a lot of residual energy in this area, but I do sense the young girl's spirit as being quite active also. It's very strong.

Because the library was getting ready to close, we didn't have the opportunity to go back inside that night to check further about the history of the area, or get to know Sir Andrew a little better, but we made a mental note to do so sometime in the very near future.

As far as the ghostly photo is concerned, the fee for using it in this book was quite prohibitive, so if you're interested in having a peek for yourself, the photograph can be found at: http://jpg1.lapl.org/pics37/00038355.jpg.

New Tales From an Old Cemetery

Victoria Gross and I met up with Hollywood historian Scott Michaels at the Hollywood Forever Cemetery one afternoon to see if we could contact any of the cemetery's restless spirits. It is one of the most haunted places in Hollywood and boasts a number of very famous ghosts, including Clifton Webb, Rudolph Valentino, and notorious mobster "Bugsy" Siegel. It was our hope that some of these famous folk might like to have a chat.

Hollywood Forever was founded as Hollywood Memorial Park Cemetery in 1899 by Hollywood denizens I. N. Van Nuys and Colonel Isaac Lankershim on 100 prime acres in the heart of Hollywood. In 1901, Mrs. Highland Price, a blacksmith's wife, was the first person to be interred at the cemetery. Since then, some of the most famous stars in the history of Hollywood, including Douglas Fairbanks, Sr., Iron Eyes Cody, Peter Lorre, Mel Blanc, Tyrone Power, and Carl "Alfalfa" Switzer have been laid to rest at Hollywood Forever. Charlie Chaplin's mother and son are also buried there, as are Anthony Quinn's infant son and Clark Gable's father, numerous Hollywood directors, producers and composers, war heroes, government officials, and a clever man named Elmer Berger who has the distinction of being the inventor of the rear-view mirror.

While we were hoping for a quiet afternoon of ghost hunting, this *is* Hollywood after all, and as we drove into the cemetery gates, we ran into more than we bargained for. The quiet cemetery streets were lined with cars and huge "Star Wagons" which are portable make-up and dressing rooms for location productions. The cemetery is often used as a backdrop for television shows and feature films. In fact, a couple of nights before our visit, I had seen an episode of *Moonlight* in which the Cathedral Mausoleum and the cemetery grounds were prominently featured.

They were actually filming two separate productions at the cemetery that day, one of which was the hit television series *Ugly Betty*.

A nearby lawn was tented and laid out with tables and chairs. This was the catering area where people were milling around taking in sustenance. The chapel, which was one of the places we'd hoped to visit was entirely closed off due to the production, as was the Columbarium, another planned stop for us.

With all this organized chaos going on, we decided to head over to the Cathedral Mausoleum at the far end of the cemetery which, thankfully, appeared to be a "production free zone" to see if we could talk to Rudolph Valentino or any of the mausoleum's other inhabitants who happened to be hanging around.

We had just walked into the mausoleum when Victoria said she kept picking up something to do with Elvis Presley. "I know he's not buried here," she said, "but I can't get Elvis Presley out of my mind. Perhaps one of his fans is buried here and is bringing the image across. Maybe we'll find out who it is a little bit later."

As we walked down a long corridor to find Valentino's crypt, Victoria felt quite a bit of energy at first, but no spirits. She said the energy was probably so strong because of the thousands of people who come from all over the world to visit the famous actor's final resting place, but then she picked up the spirit of a young man, probably twenty-five to thirty years of age who was trying hard to make his presence known.

"He's tall, has dark hair, very fair skin, and he's from back in the 1920s. He's a real character and must have been an entertainer of some sort because he is quite a jolly soul, and his laughter helps dispel any negative energy that might otherwise be around."

While this secretive soul wasn't forthcoming with a name, he did tease us by telling Victoria that he was buried close by in that section of the mausoleum.

Valentino's spirit was nowhere to be found, nor were actors Peter Finch, Larry White from *Bewitched,* or Silent Screen Goddess Barbara La Marr, who was known as "The Woman Who Was Too Beautiful."

Scott told us that David White's son, Jonathan, who also resides in the niche with his father, was killed in one of the more infamous terrorism cases of the past twenty-five years on December 21, 1988 when Pan Am Flight 103 broke apart at 13,000 feet over Lockerbee, Scotland, after an explosion ripped through the forward cargo hold. All 259 passengers and crew were killed. Investigation of the wreckage revealed fragments of explosive materials that had been detonated inside a piece of luggage.

David White and his son, Jonathan.

As we left the area and walked passed the larger-than-life statue of Saint James Minor, one of the foreboding marble statues of the Twelve Apostles which line the foyer of the mausoleum, Victoria sensed that we weren't alone.

"I'm getting chills around this statue," she said, "and I think the spirit who is here belongs to one of the people buried in one of the niches right behind it."

The interesting thing about that particular area was that there were quite a few remains with the Masonic emblem on their urns, and the Masons have always been known for their "mysterious ways."

Freemasonry exists in various forms all over the world, and has millions of members. They all share moral and metaphysical ideals, which include, in most cases, a constitutional declaration of belief in a Supreme Being. They have long been the target of conspiracy theories, and seen as an occult and evil power. While Freemasonry has often been called a "secret society," Freemasons themselves argue that it is more correct to say that it is an esoteric society, in that certain aspects are private. The most common phrasing being that Freemasonry has, in the twenty-first century, become less a secret society and more of a "society with secrets." The private aspects of modern Freemasonry are the modes of recognition amongst members and particular elements within the ritual.

Victoria said that this particular spirit, who she described as "not a particularly nice person," had no interest in talking to us and preferred to just hang around and observe, and was, for some strange reason, banging on the statue of Saint James with his fists.

James was made a martyr upon his death in Jerusalem when a Jewish high priest asked him to stand on the Temple wall and speak against Jesus to the crowds which had gathered in preparation for the Passover. James instead

Scott, Victoria, and St. James Minor.

spoke in favor of Jesus as the Christ. Many heard him and many were converted. So the Jewish religious leaders threw James down from the Temple wall. He did not die from the fall, so they began to stone him. Still he did not die from the stoning, so a man took a fuller club (used to beat out clothing) and clubbed him to death. The high priest, Ananus, rebuked the Jewish high priest for killing James and when Herod Agrippa II heard of this killing, he promptly removed the priest from office.

"Maybe this spirit is trying to use this statue as a way of going through the Pearly Gates," Victoria mused. "He's really an aggressive and dominant type, but there is no violence surrounding him, not like that the guy who resides in that crypt we passed on our way in."

She was referring to the crypt of William Deane Tanner, also known as William Desmond Taylor.

Taylor was born on April 26, 1872, and was an actor, a successful U. S. film director of silent movies, and a popular figure in the growing Hollywood film colony of the 1910s and early 1920s. On February 1, 1922, he was shot to death in his bungalow. His unsolved murder was one of Hollywood's earliest major scandals. Taylor's funeral was one of the most impressive ever held in Los Angeles. Every person of prominence in the picture industry attended the services.

Victoria continued,

"I got the impression that Tanner was a very weak man in life, while this guy is very strong."

While I thought it odd that spirits would want to hang around a cemetery when they could be popping in and out of places all over the world, Victoria explained that especially with spirits who are quite old, their mindsets are different than ours.

"In the Victorian age and at the turn of the twentieth century, many people didn't believe in an afterlife, and those who did, due to their religious beliefs, were taught about judgments, and things like that. So lots of times, they are afraid to move on and cross over to the other side; and since this was their "last space," the place where their bodies lie, they choose to stay close to their earthly remains rather than crossing over and facing the possibility that they might end up in Hell for their actions here on Earth. Or, in some cases, they just don't believe in an afterlife so they remain where the body is.

My theory was that once a person dies, they would then realize that there was an afterlife and they would normally then just cross over, but Victoria pretty much summed it up when she said, "They're not going to get to it if they don't believe it. There's a whole theory these days going on in the paranormal community that graveyards aren't haunted, but yes they are.

After we left the mausoleum, we headed across the grounds past the beautiful lake to the grave of Virginia Rappe.

In cemetery lore, her spirit has been seen numerous times kneeling in front of her grave and wailing loudly into the night.

Hollywood Forever Lake.

Virginia Rappe was a popular young starlet from 1916 until her untimely death in 1921. She also has the distinction of being the center of the biggest scandal to ever rock Hollywood during that era. Although she was ultimately discovered to have died of peritonitis caused by a ruptured bladder, it was initially allegedly that she had been raped by silent screen comic Roscoe 'Fatty' Arbuckle during a wild party at the Saint Francis Hotel in San Francisco. Arbuckle was accused of her rape and murder and brought to trial. Although he was ultimately acquitted after enduring three manslaughter trials, the scandal ruined both Arbuckle's motion picture career and his life. It is thought that Rappe's mournful spirit is seen and heard on a regular basis either because she's unhappy that she died at such a young age, or because she's angry that Arbuckle was acquitted.

Victoria pointed out that there was a very sad woman spirit who was standing alongside the grave.

At the same time, Scott pointed to the headstone adjacent to Rappe's with the name Henry Lehrman and said it belonged to a man who considered himself to be her fiancée. "He visited her grave every day, claiming to be her fiancée," said Scott, "but she didn't appear to be someone who was a one-man kind of woman when she was alive."

"She's just told me that he may have thought he was her fiancée," said Victoria, "but he definitely was not."

"I'm also going to go out on a limb here and say that Virginia is not the one people see and hear crying over her grave. "She is coming across as a strong woman and is portraying herself to me as gracious and elegant, but I think the wailer is someone else. A blond woman."

Scott then interjected that perhaps it was the spirit of Rappe's mother who is mournful and possibly regrets pushing her daughter into situations like the party in San Francisco where Rappe met her untimely death.

"There is so much doubt in this area, perhaps about the trial, of the way she met her death, but it was the mother who actually came out and accused Fatty Arbuckle of raping her daughter," said Scott.

"That could be," said Victoria, "because I really don't think Virginia Rappe is still harboring any grudges, and she's not sitting around crying about what happened. She's gone on. I personally don't feel it's her doing the haunting because she knows the truth. Victoria continued,

"Arbuckle did kill her, though, even though technically, it wasn't an intentional murder. She's telling me that the

Victoria saw the White Lady standing next to this tree.

outcome of the trial was unfair, but she's saying she's angry about having been brought into that situation in the first place and the other people involved in getting her there, perhaps her mother, rather than being angry about the way she died."

As we left Virginia Rappe's gravesite Victoria noticed the spirit of a lady dressed in white chiffon standing under a nearby tree. "There always has to be a lady in white, doesn't there?" laughed Victoria. "This lady is from around the 1800s, is in her late teens, early twenties at the most and is definitely buried near here. She's a restless soul who I think definitely haunts this place at night."

In the true spirit of a phantom, the minute we began talking about her, the spirit faded away.

Our last stop of the day was going to be a quick chat with notorious gangster Bugsy Siegel who is buried in the Beth Olam Mausoleum. Along the way, we paid our respects to director John Huston, actress Fay Wray, *Get Smart's* Don Adams and the infamous" Lady in Black," whose spirit is still seen by many hovering around Rudolph Valentino's crypt. We also came across a memorial marker (centopath) for Jayne Mansfield.

When we entered Beth Olam, Scott, who knows exactly where all of the cemetery's famous souls are buried, lead us over to the gangster's crypt, but apparently Mr. Siegel was "not at home."

Strangely enough, Victoria sensed a strong attachment to writing at Siegel's crypt, so if anyone knows anything about Bugsy Siegel the Author, please drop me a line and let me know.

There was a little girl spirit, between five to seven years old who Victoria says plays in there all the time.

"She's telling me that her name is Sarah, and I have to say that she didn't die of natural causes. I think hers was a violent death. I'm getting the impression that she was kidnapped and murdered, but she must feel very loved around here, because she said that she's here all the time. And there's also a little boy with her, but it's her spirit who stands out quite strongly. I think she's from the 1950s.

"I think she remains here because of the atmosphere. It feels very nurturing in here, and if I were a young

JOHN HUSTON
1906 - 1987

BELOVED MOTHER
RHEA HUSTON
1882 - 1938

FAY WRAY
1907 - 2004

spirit, where else would I go other than a place where I could feel mothered, protected, and safe? A place full of Jewish mothers."

On our way out of the cemetery, we stopped to tape a quick publicity promo for my book. We thought it would be appropriate to use the cemetery grounds as a backdrop and decided to use two or three different locations to see which would look best on camera.

After the first two "takes," we moved over to a spot where the tombstones were quite dense and there was a lovely tree right behind me. I stood behind one of the tombstones and rested my arms on it. When the camera started rolling and I began to talk; all of a sudden, I found myself having trouble breathing and there was a tightness in my chest. As soon as I stepped away from the headstone, though, I felt perfectly fine. Could it have been that the owner of the tombstone was someone who passed away from heart or breathing problems and was trying to physically relate those details to me?

Since there is no way of finding out, I guess that incident will remain one of Hollywood Forever's many hidden secrets.

Come On–A My (Haunted) House

Ghosts remind me about men's smart crack about women, you can't live with then and you can't live without them.

—Eugene O'Neill

Rosemary Clooney was a popular singer and actress. She is best known for performing pop music in the 1940s and 1950s with songs like "Come On-a My House" and starred in dozens of movies such as, *White Christmas* with Bing Crosby. Crosby was once quoted as saying that Clooney was "the best in the business."

In 1956, she starred in her own a half-hour syndicated television musical variety show, *The Rosemary Clooney Show*. The show featured the "Hi-Lo's" singing group and "Nelson Riddle's Orchestra." The following year, the show moved to NBC prime time as *The Lux Show Starring Rosemary Clooney.*

In her personal life, Clooney was married three times, twice to José Ferrer (from 1953 until 1961 and again from 1964 to 1967). Ferrer was an Academy Award-winning actor and film director. He first became famous on Broadway in 1935, then made his film debut with Ingrid Bergman in *Joan of Arc* in 1948, for which he received his first Academy Award nomination, for Best Supporting Actor. Ferrer won an Academy Award as Best Actor for his portrayal of Cyrano de Bergerac in the 1950 film version of *Cyrano de Bergerac* only weeks after being subpoenaed to appear before the House UnAmerican Activities Committee as a suspected Communist, charges that Ferrer vehemently denied. In later years, Ferrer had a recurring role as Julia Duffy's insanely wealthy WASPy father on the popular *Newhart* television sitcom in the U.S. in the 1980s. He also had a memorable recurring role as elegant and flamboyant attorney Reuben Marino on the soap opera *Another World* in the early 1980s. He narrated the very first episode of the popular 1964 sitcom *Bewitched*, in mock documentary style.

Clooney and Ferrer had five children together and the pressure of raising a large brood while pursuing careers as television, movie, radio, and recording stars was a tough life to live and their marriage began to deteriorate. The stress soon took its toll and Clooney developed an addiction to tranquilizers and sleeping pills. Although her life appeared idyllic to the public, the singer's addiction to drugs worsened. Recalling in her autobiography how she fell prey to "the '50s myth of family and career," the singer confessed, "I just did it all because I thought that I could. It certainly wasn't easy."

As if her life wasn't tough enough, Clooney was present at the 1968 assassination of her close friend, Robert F. Kennedy. She was standing only yards away from Kennedy who was shot while campaigning for the Democratic presidential nomination at the Ambassador Hotel in Los Angeles. The tragedy, compounded with her drug addiction, triggered a public mental collapse. At a Reno, Nevada, engagement shortly thereafter, she cursed at her audience and stalked off the stage. She later called a press conference to announce her retirement at which she sobbed incoherently. When a doctor was summoned, Clooney fled and was eventually found driving on the wrong side of a dangerous mountain road. Soon thereafter she admitted herself to the psychiatric ward of Mount Sinai Hospital in Los Angeles. Clooney remained in therapy for many years. She worked when she could—at Holiday Inns and small hotels like the Ventura and the Hawthorne and selling paper towels in television commercials.

In 1976, Clooney's old friend, Bing Crosby, asked her to join him on his 50th anniversary tour. It would be Crosby's final tour and Clooney's comeback event. The highlight of the show came when Clooney joined Crosby in a duet of "On a Slow Boat to China." The following year, Clooney signed a recording contract with Concord Jazz, taking the next step on her comeback trail. Beginning in 1977, she recorded an album a year for Concord Records, which continued until her death. This made her something of an anomaly, because most of her generation of singers had long since stopped recording regularly by then. Clooney received the Grammy Lifetime Achievement Award in 2002.

A longtime smoker, Clooney was diagnosed with lung cancer at the end of 2001, and despite surgery, she died six months later at her home in Beverly Hills, California. At the time, she was married to her longtime companion, Dante DiPaolo, a former Hollywood dancer. They married in November of 1997. The two met on the set of the film *Here Come the Girls* (where, he said, he "fell in love" with Clooney), and continued their acquaintance during taping of the 1954 film classic *White Christmas*. But DiPaolo ultimately quit that picture to perform in another fifties movie musical, *Seven Brides for Seven Brothers* and that ended the relationship—or so it seemed.

In 1973, DiPaolo was sitting in his 1956 Thunderbird at a Beverly Hills stop light when Clooney pulled up next to him in her Corvette. They honked at each other, and Clooney yelled her phone number to DiPaolo, who wrote the number in the dust on his car's dashboard. A lasting romance ensued, and after twenty-four years as a couple, they finally made it legal.

Clooney's nephew, actor George Clooney, served as a pall bearer at her funeral, which was attended by numerous stars including Al Pacino. Clooney is buried at Saint Patrick's Cemetery, Maysville, Mason County, Kentucky.

Rosemary Clooney's very haunted Beverly Hills home was constructed for (or by) actor Monte Blue around 1928. The house contained eight bedrooms, six bathrooms, a basement, breakfast room, sun room, den, dining room, family room, living room, and covered patio.

Actor Russ Columbo lived in the house from 1932 until his tragic death in 1934. On September 2nd of that year, Columbo was shot under peculiar circumstances by his longtime friend, photographer Lansing Brown. Columbo was visiting him at the studio one day. In lighting a cigarette, Brown lit the match by striking it against the wooden stock of an antique French dueling pistol. The flame set off a long-forgotten charge in the gun, and a lead pistol ball was fired. The pistol ball ricocheted off a nearby table and hit Columbo in the left eye, killing him almost instantly. Columbo's death was ruled an accident, and Brown exonerated from blame. Columbo's lover at the time, Carole Lombard, was devastated at the news of the shooting.

From 1936-1937, composer George Gershwin, author of famous works like *Rhapsody in Blue* and *An American in Paris* and his lyricist brother Ira, author of famous works like *I Got Rhythm* and *They Can't Take That Away from Me* moved in. When George died on July 11, 1937, while working on the score of *The Goldwyn Follies* and following surgery for a brain tumor at the age of thirty-eight, Ira and his wife did not remain in the house for long. They eventually bought the house next door and lived there until they both died in that house.

Jose Ferrer and Rosemary Clooney took up residence in August of 1953, and Clooney lived in the house until her death.

Paranormal investigators Robert and Anne Wlodarski have written a great many books on the subject of ghosts and hauntings. The following information about their investigation of the Clooney house has been excerpted with permission from their upcoming book, *Spirits Live: Talking*

*with the Dead, Investigations of the International Paranormal
Research Organization.*

Upon entering the house for the first time in 2003,
Wlodarsku said the atmosphere "was as cold as a tomb" and
they were greeted by the spirits of Ira Gershwin, Rosemary
Clooney, Russ Colombo, and a few others.

"In the living room, you could feel the energy
overwhelming you. There was a sense of being watched as
well as someone playing the piano. No doubt, an afterlife
party was going on as we stood in the room—it was that
"alive" with energy and so was the back yard. When we were
standing outside by the pool I looked back at the house and
saw someone in the house on the left-hand side, peering
out of the second-floor window at us. It was a woman with
blonde hair, probably about twenty-nine to thirty years old,
with a buster-brown or mop-like hair. The cut was shorter
in the front than in the back. Actually, there was a bun in
the back. The woman was peering out when I noticed a
child next to her. He's a boy, not a child, but rather around
ten to eleven years old. He had dark hair and the woman
had her arm around him. This was on the northwest wing
of the house, second floor, over the kitchen.

"We then went into the maid's quarters and got the
sense that an older black lady occupied this area, and that
she was part of the staff here at one time. Rosemary was
right by us, watching and checking us out the entire time.
She seems to be in total charge of the spirit world inside
the house. She is not stuck, but loves the place, and so she
remains behind, as a kind of caretaker."

Light anomalies picked up in the Rosemary Clooney house.

In September 2004, the group went back and conducted a séance lead by mediums Ginny McGovern, Victoria Gross, and a couple guests, none of which had been given any information about the house or its occupants...living or dead.

After McGovern conducted an opening prayer, the séance began.

"I'm hearing very strongly, a woman's voice singing 'Fly me to the moon and let me play among the stars!' I don't know whose song that is, but I'm hearing that very strongly. This person can sing, unlike me," said Ginny, almost immediately. "So much music in this house. Oh, I'm just hearing so much music. I'm hearing mostly a woman singing. I'm hearing a record player and it's like the scratchy sounds coming through. You just don't hear it these days anymore because people have CDs."

Victoria was also picking up energy.

"I have somebody here who is very serious. He was very quiet and serious. He's about thirty... thirty to forty, thirty-eight, around there. Tall, and he's got black hair, kind of pushed back. I think it is the man I just saw the picture of, Russ Columbo. I feel a real seriousness here, though I'm not sure if that's his personality or what (moaning on the tape)... But there's a real lot, Oh my God, just real love of ... and he's wanting to say too, that there's secretness, and something is hidden. It's in the downstairs wall. Something's hidden down there, and it's valuable papers and jewels. It's more papers, but I do see some jewels. But not like mega-wise. Actually, it may have only been valuable to him. Like a family heirloom. But there is something there. And I do pick him up as being real serious and how sad he is, because he didn't mean to do this... his death. It wasn't supposed to happen like that. But he is around here. He's the guardian I saw earlier at the front door, out on the front porch, and he guards this place. He does come in and out. He's crossed over so he's not stuck. He does come in and out. He's very encouraging. I have smelled the men's cologne really strong which I said earlier during the summary session. I am smelling the cologne again. Yes, he's around. The spirits like that we are here today, because it is a party atmosphere, and they are concerned about what's going on.

"He just left."

Throughout the course of the séance, several spirits made an appearance, most notably Rosemary Clooney and her husband, Jose Ferrer. The following are the transcripts of the conversations with those two sprightly spirits.

Rosemary Clooney

Ginny McGovern: I'm getting a woman telling me about a Dalmatian, dog. Which is not a dog I was getting upstairs earlier. But this is a large Dalmatian.

Anne Wlodarski: I'm getting... what do you call those huge dogs.

Robert Wlodarski: A great Dane?

Ginny McGovern: No, this is a Dalmatian. I think its Rose…. Rosemary, telling me about the Dalmatian. So, I would be curious to know if they had Dalmatian at some time or another. She keeps telling me about the happy times, when she was young, and they really were very much in love.

Ginny McGovern: They had a lot of good times in here. Before the dark times.

Anne Wlodarski: When it got dark, it really got dark.

Ginny McGovern: It did, didn't it? I think she's referring to not only the problems of the husband, but also her illness, which was the darker, dark times. Even darker so.

Anne Wlodarski: The drug problem. Depression.

Ginny McGovern: That she had? Was this Rosemary's problem?

Anne Wlodarski: [*channeling Rosemary Clooney*] Yes. Jose, Jose can you see? You can't. You never do.

Ginny McGovern: But in the beginning it was wonderful, wasn't it!

Anne Wlodarski: [*channeling Rosemary Clooney*] It was the best.

Ginny McGovern: Is that the romantic feeling I had upstairs in the bedroom?

Anne Wlodarski: [*channeling Rosemary Clooney*] Absolutely (click on tape?)

Ginny McGovern: A lot of love between the couple.

Anne Wlodarski: [*channeling Rosemary Clooney*] Oh boy.

Ginny McGovern: What was your favorite place in the house?

Anne Wlodarski: [*channeling Rosemary Clooney*] Well, besides that room (bedroom?), the room with the piano.

Ginny McGovern: The studio upstairs?

Anne Wlodarski: [*channeling Rosemary Clooney*] Jose, Jose liked the upstairs. I liked the downstairs.

Ginny McGovern: The living room?

Anne Wlodarski: [*channeling Rosemary Clooney*] Yes.

Ginny McGovern: Was Jose a musician?

Anne Wlodarski: [*channeling Rosemary Clooney*] No. But he thought he was a singer. He tried too hard, but not with me, not nearly enough with me.

Ginny McGovern: But come on, you'd be a really hard act to follow as far as the singing.

Anne Wlodarski: [*channeling Rosemary Clooney*] Yes, I guess that's what he thought, too.

Ginny McGovern: Are you happy that we are all here today?

Anne Wlodarski: [*channeling Rosemary Clooney*] Very much so. I love to have people in the house. That's what this house was for. But mainly, it took my mind off my problems.

Ginny McGovern: The house did, or the parties?

Anne Wlodarski: [*channeling Rosemary Clooney*] Both, both! I had so much responsibility. In decorating, and what not you know. And then having baby after baby, after baby, to keep…

Ginny McGovern: How many children did you have?

Anne Wlodarski: [*channeling Rosemary Clooney*] Well, there would have been seven, but I only had five. Which turned out to be quite a handful and quite a lot. I could have had twenty-five and it wouldn't have made any difference. Jose would have strayed anyway (A discernable click on the tape). And I did think that it was my fault but it was not my fault.

Ginny McGovern: That's right. It wasn't.

Anne Wlodarski: [*channeling Rosemary Clooney*] It's not my fault.

Robert Wlodarski: There's not much you can do with those Latins. Did Lucille Ball and you every talk about your husbands?

Anne Wlodarski: [*channeling Rosemary Clooney*] We did. We were in very similar situations. And even the two divorces, you know.

Ginny McGovern: Very similar.

Anne Wlodarski: [*channeling Rosemary Clooney*] We were going back and forth. Knowing that it wouldn't work but for the children's sake. Everything was done for somebody else. For somebody else's sake, but never mine.

Robert Wlodarski: She said on her death bed that she still loved Desi, did you feel that way about Jose?

Anne Wlodarski: [*channeling Rosemary Clooney*] Yes, but it was a no-win situation as they say today (**two loud clicking sounds can be heard on the tape at this point**).

Robert Wlodarski: You know, the psychics here today were curious about, toward the end…. Did you spend a lot of time in what is called the dining room downstairs, facing out?

Anne Wlodarski: [*channeling Rosemary Clooney*] Yes. I looked out the window but I also looked out there and was very sad. It used to be a happy room for me (**a single audible click**).

Ginny McGovern: Did they make you a bedroom down there; at the end? Or did you stay upstairs?

Anne Wlodarski: [*channeling Rosemary Clooney*] There was a bed, makeshift downstairs.

Ginny McGovern: In the dining room area?

Anne Wlodarski: [*channeling Rosemary Clooney*] Yeah.

Ginny McGovern: That's what I thought.

Robert Wlodarski: Did you also stay in here and look out at your olive tree?

Anne Wlodarski: [*channeling Rosemary Clooney*] Oh that (loud clicking sound) tree. Countless memories I have. Some of the happiest were under that tree. It looks kind of bad now.

Ginny McGovern: They'll work on that.

Anne Wlodarski: [*channeling Rosemary Clooney*] It needs to be taken care of. It was such a beautiful yard.

Ginny McGovern: Lisa said that they would have an arborist come and look at the tree. Would that make you happy?

Anne Wlodarski: [*channeling Rosemary Clooney*] It would make the tree happy.

Ginny McGovern: [*group laughing*] Yes it would.

Anne Wlodarski: [*channeling Rosemary Clooney*] I hated leaving here. I hated leaving my families' house.

Ginny McGovern: Now you come and visit when you want to; Don't you?

Anne Wlodarski: [*channeling Rosemary Clooney*] Yeah, but it's not the same. There are still people here, and I see old friends, but sometimes, they don't see me.

Ginny McGovern: Is there anything specifically that you'd like us to do while we're here?

Anne Wlodarski: [*channeling Rosemary Clooney*] Have a good time. To bad you didn't bring any booze with you [*people laugh*]

Ginny McGovern: No, we didn't.

Anne Wlodarski: [*channeling Rosemary Clooney*] We would have a party like this in the good old days.

Ginny McGovern: I'm sure they will have parties here.

Anne Wlodarski: [*channeling Rosemary Clooney*] Have a couple martinis. Well, that's all I have to say. I think I'll go. I'm so...

Ginny McGovern: Could we ask if anyone has a question?

Guest: She's still singing.

Ginny McGovern: She is definitely still singing.

Anne Wlodarski: [*channeling Rosemary Clooney*] That's where I want to go.

Ginny McGovern: I bet your voice is absolutely gorgeous up there, too.. over there.

Anne Wlodarski: [*channeling Rosemary Clooney*] Well, thank you very much!

Ginny McGovern: Thank you.

Anne Wlodarski: [*channeling Rosemary Clooney*] ... [*Singing while hand is tapping on the table*] Why don't you come over to my house... Why don't you come over to my house. That was my Italian song with pigeon English.

Ginny McGovern: Victoria, what do you have? (*voice on tape says something like case, okay...???*)

(Victoria Gross) Nothing.

Guest: *Doesn't it feel different now?*

Ginny McGovern: Yes. The energies... Yes, it was like, boom. Did you feel it too?

Guest: *... it feels different now.*

Jose Ferrer

Anne Wlodarski: [*channeling*] I am a man in this house and I'm not sure who I am.

Guest: You're no sure who you are?

Anne Wlodarski: [*channeling*] No, I am not sure.

Ginny McGovern: Did you live in this house?

Anne Wlodarski: [*channeling*] [*emphatic*] Yes I did.

Guest: *I was going to say, it's Jose! I heard someone say Jose.*

Ginny McGovern: Is this Jose? (an odd ha or ahh in a woman's voice, different from Anne's can be heard)

Anne Wlodarski: [*channeling*] It's hard to say, but I'm Jose [laughter around the room]

Ginny McGovern: Okay, I'm Jose.

Guest: *I, yi, yi.*

Anne Wlodarski: [*channeling*] I, yi, yi, yi, yi! Selma.

Guest: *Yes.*

Anne Wlodarski: Answer the question.

Guest: *I have to think about it… I mean, I do believe…*

Anne Wlodarski: [*channeling*] Not with your head… Come on, give me something! Give me something girl!

Guest: *He'll never go away if you don't.*

Anne Wlodarski: [*channeling*] I'll follow you home.

Ginny McGovern: Did you hear what he just said. He said 'I'll follow you home.'

Guest: *He'll follow me home?*

Ginny McGovern: He wants you to understand basically… would you mind Jose if I say this… He wants you to understand that there's no accident that you guys got this house… and with that, understanding comes a responsibility.

Anne Wlodarski: [*channeling*] You know it baby.

Ginny McGovern: And Jose understands, that it is now your home, and you may do with it as you wish, providing that you communicate with them, and you respect them as well as they'll respect you. They know there needs to be changes… modern times, things change, that's okay… and I think they will cooperate with you that way, as long as your respectful of them. But, that said, the important part is that you need to understand that there are no accidents, and….

Anne Wlodarski: [*channeling*] Does she understand that?

Ginny McGovern: I think so.

Guest: *It's hard to absorb this… it really is…*

Anne Wlodarski: [*channeling*] Absorb it… absorb it… it's here.

Ginny McGovern: Okay, but…

Guest: Give her time… okay.

Guest: Can you tell what her responsibility is… What is the responsibility? You're saying they have a responsibility. But what is the responsibility. Why was it important that the Fischs get this?

Anne Wlodarski: [*channeling*] My Rosie. I just want somebody to appreciate it as much as I did… as much as we all did…

Ginny McGovern: I think the fact that we're all here, talking with you right now, shows that they do appreciate it a lot.

Anne Wlodarski: [*channeling*] I'm not convinced. At any rate, you know, you gotta do whatcha gotta do. But, I like to be happy, and I hope you make me happy.

Ginny McGovern: But you understand now, that it's their home… Come on..

Anne Wlodarski: [*channeling*] Yeah, yeah, yeah, yeah…

Ginny McGovern: That's only fair.

Anne Wlodarski: [*channeling*] But, you know… think about it, think about it… responsibility, integrity…

Ginny McGovern: Understood..

Anne Wlodarski: [*channeling*] And, follow your hearts… your hearts' desires. You know, not… and I'm talking to Selma now.. not any other of her family. Follow your heart… don't let anybody else tell you what to do… and, you know, if you want to tear this place down, and that's in your heart of hearts, do it. But if it's not, don't do that… and you'll know what to do… you'll know what to do… Adios amigos….

Ginny McGovern: Thank you, Jose.

Back to Boardner's Bar

"The murdered do haunt their murderers, I believe…"

—Emily Bronte, *Wuthering Heights*

When I investigated Boardner's bar in Hollywood for my first paranormal book, we picked up on quite a few lively spirits. Because there was so much activity there, it was decided that we would return one day and do a séance.

It took a few months to get back to Boarnder's, but one afternoon psychic medium Michael J. Kouri called and asked if I was free to go on a "Michael Adventure" with him. He needed to take a few pictures around Hollywood for one of his upcoming ghost books, and an adventure sounded like fun.

After a tense moment or two at a nearby Hollywood park, where a bust of Rudolph Valentino was keeping company with

a few rather scary older men who were clearly in a "mind-altered state," Michael suggested we stop by Boardner's as he had not been with me on the first investigation and wanted to kind of get a feel of the place in preparation for our upcoming séance.

As I wrote in my first book, Boardner's is a local hangout for the "Who's Who & Who Cares." It has been one of Hollywood's best kept secrets since 1942. Visiting Boardner's is like taking a step back in time and the ghosts of its storied past are evident the minute you walk through the door. With it's black leather booths and dim lighting, the atmosphere is very reminiscent of the 1940s and a sense of Old Hollywood is definitely in the air. Folks Errol Flynn, Phil Harris and Alice Faye, George Gobel,

One of the stairways up to the loft.

Pat O'Brien, Lucille Ball, and many others wined and dined at the tavern after a hard day's work. Today, a younger crowd prevails, and on weekends, the bar transforms itself into Bar Sinister, a hangout for the local Goth crowd.

When Michael and I arrived unannounced, we learned that the bar's owner, Tricia La Belle, wasn't there, but the bartender was kind enough to let us go exploring on our own.

Boardner's is divided into three sections. When you first walk in the door, there is a bar and dining room where the weekday crowd hang out. Along a corridor at the far end of the dining room, patrons have access to an outside courtyard, and just to the left of the main bar is a cavernous room and loft that opens up on the weekends for Bar Sinister. The bartender let us in there so we could go and check out that area, because the upstairs loft is one of the most haunted places in the building.

The huge room was quite dark and gave off a rather eerie feeling as Michael and I made our way to the loft.

"It's quite active up here," he said after walking around for a moment. "I'm picking up the spirit of a man named Harold, who was a friend of the previous owner, and also a young woman named Sally.

Sally told Michael that she was part of the Bar Sinister crowd and that she died in a car accident a few years ago. She said she hangs around Boardner's because she really liked the place when she was alive and still comes in quite often."

"She's telling me that someone recently fell down the stairs," said Michael, pointing to one of the steep staircases that lead up to the loft. "They weren't badly hurt, though, and she also says that everyone jokingly refers to the loft as the 'Coke Den' even though that doesn't happen to be the case."

When Michael and I walked back downstairs, Sally followed.

"She says she really likes your energy," Michael told me, and then she proceeded to tell him about an unfortunate incident that happened in the area in the 1950s when a woman was brutally raped at knife point by five men.

"She says they were gangster-types and after they finished their brutal assault, they left the poor woman for dead."

As Michael was relaying this to me, we both heard what sounded like someone coming into the room, going behind the bar and knocking some of the glasses about. Thinking that the bartender from the other room had come in to get something, we both turned around at the same time to see who was there, but nobody was behind the bar.

"That was Harold," said Michael, who was quite pleased with the phenomenon. "He's just letting us know that he's still here. I'm getting the impression that he was quite a womanizer in his day, and it seems that he's quite taken by you," he chuckled.

Having never been "hit on" by a ghost before, I wasn't sure how to respond, so I just acknowledged the compliment and as it was getting late and Michael had another appointment, we quickly finished our impromptu investigation and called it a night.

Interestingly enough, I spoke to Michael several days later and he mentioned that Harold had actually followed him home from Boardner's the night we were there. "He's just lonely," explained Michael in Harold's defense.

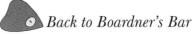

We had arranged to conduct the séance the following week, and on the appointed afternoon, we met Tricia

at the bar. Hollywood historian Scott Michaels also joined us, as did Michael's publicist and a few others.

Because Michael feels that energy should be distributed equally among the séance participants, we gathered around the table and he showed us where he would like each of us to sit. He then placed several objects on the table including a candle which would be used for spirit communication and some personal objects from some of Hollywood's most famous stars.

He brought along a tie and tie clip that once belonged to Douglas Fairbanks, Sr. who was

Sally's Loft.

Psychic Michael J. Kouri

married to Mary Pickford. "I read something in a book about Mary Pickford," Michael explained, "and in it she talked about Boarnder's and having dinner here." An obvious connection.

He also brought a broach that belonged to Mae West which was worn during the filming of *Diamond Lil,* a green bracelet that Agnes Moorehead wore as part of her prop jewelry while portraying Endora on *Bewitched,* a military piece that belonged to actor Ramon Navarro, which actually came from a World War I hat, but was used in one of his movies as well. There was also a Bakelite sweater clip that belonged to Joan Crawford, a bolo tie with a silver dollar in the center which was once Rudolph Valentino's. The tie was given to him by Natacha Rambova. The last piece of jewelry that he laid out on the table was a rhinestone headdress that belonged to Clara Bow, one of Hollywood's most famous (and notorious) Silent Screen actresses and known at the time as The "It" Girl.

Michael advised,

"I brought these items because spirits are often attached to objects they owned during their lifetime and I'm hoping that some of them will join us here today."

After everyone examined the artifacts and we were all in our seats, we were ready to get started.

"I'm going ask God to protect all of us," said Michael, and then after we were told to take a few cleansing breaths, he had us visualize entering our own protective pink bubble. Then we were instructed to join hands in order to create a circle of energy, and the séance began.

"Many spirits will communicate with us by means of the candle flame," Michael explained, "while others will talk to me directly. Right now I want you to think about people that you want to talk to, maybe a family member or perhaps someone famous. Thinking about them will help bring their energy forward. And I'd also like to tell you that while we were doing the meditation, I could see all of your auras and all of your spirit guides. There are about eighteen spirits with us right

Celebrity memorabilia on the table,
and a strange white streak on the bench that could not be seen with the naked eye.

now. They're standing all around us and they're eager to speak. Some of them are celebrities and some are people you've never heard of before, but it's going to be very interesting."

"By the way, Scott," he added, "did you know that you have five spirits around you? I saw them when you first came in and shook your hand. When you enter a room, you come in with an entourage."

As Michael went around the table asking participants if they had any questions for spirit, several entities immediately came through, many of them family members of the participants and Michael passed along the messages they had to convey to their loved ones, but it wasn't long before the Hollywood procession began.

Back to Boardner's Bar 171

Mae West, Rudolph Valentino, Ramon Novarro, and Anna Nicole Smith all gave signs of being in attendance. Michael explained that Mae comes to him quite often and she's always a pleasure to talk to.

When Michael asked if anyone had any questions for Mae, Scott couldn't help asking the question that had been whispered about the screen goddess quite often. To put it delicately, it alluded to the theory that Mae West was actually a man. This rumor no doubt came about because of the actresses' "drag queen persona" and bawdy sense of humor. When asked, the question didn't seem to ruffle Miss West's feathers at all.

"I was all woman," she drawled in response, and then, as if to prove her point, she let us in on a few personal bits of information that are better left unrepeated here.

Michael then spoke of a rather angry spirit named Albert who had just joined us and wanted to be heard.

"I'm getting the name Albert very strong," said Michael. "And there's something very odd about him. He has a slight mustache, very thin, and there's a strange tattoo on his throat, and it's in red. I can't make out what it says, but it's very thick and almost like it isn't a tattoo at all, but some kind of makeup or something. He's wearing a suit and his shirt is kind of open, no tie, and he looks like he's from the 1940s or 50s. I also see a woman dressed like a dominatrix standing next to him. Albert is about 5'9" or 5'10" in height and his hair looks sort of like light brown and wavy. His face is sort of square."

Both Scott and I were interested in finding out more about Albert because we thought we might know who he was, so without giving anything away, I asked Michael if this man had ever lived on Normandie Avenue in Hollywood. Michael gave us confirmation that he had.

We suspected that this might be the spirit of film actor Albert Dekker, who was best known for his roles in *Dr. Cyclops*, *The Killers*, *East of Eden*, and *The Wild Bunch*. He had also been a former California Legislator. During the McCarthy era, Dekker became an outspoken critic of the Wisconsin senator's tactics, and as a result found it hard to get work in Hollywood. When he publicly denounced the red-baiting McCarthy, calling him "insane," he began receiving death threats and he was blacklisted in the Hollywood community. He returned to Broadway, then made a movie comeback in 1959. During his last decade, Dekker alternated between film, stage, and TV assignments and also embarked on several college-campus lecture tours.

But these days, Dekker is best know for his grotesquely strange death rather than his accomplishments in life. The story of his passing began to unfold on May 5, 1968, in the actor's apartment on Normandie Avenue.

After attempting to reach Dekker for three days, his fiancé, Geraldine Saunders, got worried and went to the actor's home where she found numerous messages and notes from concerned friends attached to his door. She summoned the building manager and expressed her concern and asked him to open the door.

Once inside, they searched the apartment and came upon a horrific sight in the bathroom when they found Dekker's dead body kneeling nude in the bathtub with a noose around his neck and a scarf tied over his eyes. A horse's bit, fashioned from a rubber ball and metal wire were in his mouth with two leather straps stretched between the leather belts that girded his neck and chest. A third belt, around his waist, was tied with a rope that stretched to his ankles. The end of the rope was found wrapped around his wrist several times and was held in Dekker's hand. Handcuffs were on both wrists with a key attached and Dekker also had sexually explicit writings and drawings, written in red lipstick, on various parts of his body. It was later determined that he had been dead for several days. He was sixty-two years old.

Reports surfaced that Dekker was the victim of a robbery gone wrong due to a great deal of cash and electronic equipment that was found to be missing from his apartment, but there was no evidence to support this. Police also theorized that Dekker was a closet homosexual who practiced his eccentricities discreetly with anonymous male prostitutes. Police attempted to attribute Dekker's death to a mishap with a hustler who left the actor dying or dead after something went horribly wrong.

Police made inquiries, but the actor had no reputation among male hustlers and Dekker's friends denied the accusations. Other theories of a murder made to look like a suicide arose but were never proven, and during the brief investigation, detectives noted that there were no signs of forced entry or a struggle. And, if Dekker had been alone, how could he have legibly written on his own backside?

Albert Dekker's death was eventually ruled accidental. The coroner determined that Dekker accidentally asphyxiated himself while attempting autoerotic asphyxia and while the case was then closed to further inquiry, the circumstances surrounding the actor's death remained a mystery all these years. But it seems that the spirit of Albert Dekker is not at all satisfied with the outcome of the investigation, and might have come to us to set the story straight.

"He's saying to me something about, 'She did it,'" said Michael. "He's also saying that people have made fun about him after his death and he's very unhappy about that."

At that point, Michael asked us if what he had just said meant anything to anyone. Scott spoke up and said that what Michael was relaying sounded like he was talking about Albert Dekker. When Michael asked for confirmation as to whether the spirit actually was Dekker, he got a positive response when our séance table began to move about on its own.

"I see something in his back, like a knife, but that's not how he died." Michael continued, "I think it's symbolic because he's telling me that people had stabbed him in the back during his lifetime and he's showing me this because it's a way of letting me know what he is feeling. He's also giving me the name Dominique and saying that she was involved in his death, and that there was a great deal of money missing from his apartment."

"He says that he was drugged and is saying methanol." (The police confirmed that he'd been injected with a drug, but after three days it was unidentifiable.) "He's telling me he was tied up, handcuffed and had cuffs on his ankles, and he's saying something about that (obscenity) Noguchi deeming his death a suicide."

Thomas Noguchi is a former Chief Medical Examiner-Coroner for the County of Los Angeles. He served in that position from 1967 to 1982. Known as the "coroner to the stars," he determined the cause of death in many high profile cases, including Albert Dekker's.

"Albert is saying, 'It was not a suicide, I was murdered, and how the (obscenity) could they deem it a suicide because I was hogtied, and how can one person hogtie themselves in that way?'

"He says that they also stole a very expensive camera of his as well as cash."

At this point, the candle flame began flickering wildly, indicating that the spirit was quite upset and the table continued to move. Because the spirit was in obvious distress, Michael asked if there was anything he could do to help.

"He is saying, 'You can get the bastards that did this to me and ruined my family's name. She's old now, but the woman who did this to me is still alive.' One of them lives in the Knickerbocker Hotel right now, he says, and since that hotel was converted into a senior citizen's complex in recent years, that does make sense.

"He says this has really put a damper on his children's lives and that they really can't be at rest because they don't really know what happened to him and they're totally embarrassed. He also says his fiancée was never the same after seeing him like that and he wants justice."

Michael then asked Albert whether he had been known for hiring hookers.

"He says, 'I wouldn't exactly call her that, but let's just say she took care of things my fiancée wouldn't do.'"

Then he asked Albert if he had been into bondage and he said no, they'd never done anything like that before.

Scott then asked if Dekker knew what had happened to his earthly remains because it is known that he was cremated, but their whereabouts is unknown.

Just before the séance began, we picked up this orb hovering above the table. Some people claim to see a face in it that resembles Albert Dekker.

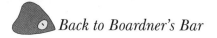

"He says no, and he wants to find that out as well," said Michael. "He says that you might want to ask his daughter. Maybe she has them."

At that point, having said what needed to be said, Albert's energy faded away.

Michael called me the next day and said that Albert came to him later that evening and asked that both Scott and I do whatever we can to help clear his name. Hopefully, talking about the séance in this book might bring someone forward who knows about the case and the actor's tortured soul may finally get some closure.

Michael J. Kouri Speaks Out: Hearing Bugles and Doors

People fear death even more than pain. It's strange that they fear death.
Life hurts a lot more than death. At the point of death, the pain is over.
Yeah, I guess it is a friend.

—Jim Morrison

Throughout my career as a Psychic-Medium and Parapsychological Investigator, I've come to know and understand what *ghosts* really are and why they choose to remain here on the earth along with the living after their lives are over. There are as many different types of ghosts as there are people of multiple nationalities and each situation is just as different as those in our lives, too. There are spirits of people who have died quickly and tragically and don't even know they've left their earthly vessels (their bodies) and those who do acknowledge they are now in spirit, but had some unfinished business such as a divorce, the sale of their home, their antique collection, or they simply feel the need to stay around to make sure their loved one's are taken care of. (Especially if the deceased was the main caregiver.) Then there are the spiritual entities who wreak havoc over us as they did in their own lives.

You see, to me, the spirits I've encountered throughout my career seem to do the same things they did in life and it would seem to those who actually live among the spirits that these specters of light and darkness always appear to be doing the same type of antics, perhaps just to get our attention. When I enter a haunted place (and I have to tell you that the word *haunted* doesn't mean *scary;* it means there is a presence around you), I can see these spirits flipping off light switches, or television sets, or CD and stereo systems so as not to waste electricity just as they did in life, or when I see them cooking at a large stove in a kitchen, I realize that in their lifetime in this place, the room they appear in was their kitchen, which in this time period could be the operating room of a hospital built over the exact site of a home that stood years before.

Most of the haunting experiences I've encountered during the past twenty-eight years are logical and make perfect sense to those who can understand it, however I often encounter skeptical people who can't understand why spirits would remain on the earth plane after death. And there are those people who don't want to believe anything that's not proven to them in a physical way. In truth, I don't care if other people don't believe in this, because I know what *I've encountered*, seen, heard, and touched throughout *my life* and this is what is real *to me.*

I often talk about my personal encounters with these unseen specters of light and sound that millions of people from all walks of life and religious beliefs, claim to have witnessed themselves. Today, in the twenty-first century, we've seen the television docudramas being produced about mediums, how they help the dead and the living to figure out where to go and how to deal with their ghostly situations. We've seen motion pictures like *The Sixth Sense* and *The Others*. Hollywood producers and writers seem to be doing their homework by studying and researching books like mine and those who've written before me and that's what I call Hollywood evolution.

So when I encounter skeptical people who ask me about these paranormal situations, I throw back the question, "What's not to believe?" Search for the answers of the questions of your own life path and don't just rely on the tabloids, the movies, and other fanatical ideals—search for the truth for yourself.

To the date of this publication, I've written twenty-seven books on the subject of my personal Parapsychological adventures, and throughout my career, I've investigated thousands of so called *haunted* sites. Stop by my web site at www.icghosts.com to learn more about my background, books, and Hollywood's spirits!

In the meantime, read on to gain some perspective into some of Hollywood's greats!

Montgomery Clift

Montgomery Clift does still reside in room 928, the room he called home at the Hollywood Roosevelt Hotel where he lived for several weeks while filming the 1953 hit *From Here To Eternity*. Back in the fall of 1988, a group of psychic friends and I rented that room for two nights while we investigated several haunted hot spots in Hollywood area to see if what we'd read in other books could possibly be true, that the Hollywood Roosevelt Hotel was indeed the most haunted hotel of them all. A few of the psychics I'd invited to join me suggested we hold a Communication Circle (séance) in the room to see who might come through from the other side. Since this hotel has the reputation as being one of the most truly haunted hot spots in tinseltown, we decided we'd let our own psychic gifts lead the way into the afterlife and see if any of these famous ghouls were floating around while we were there. We decided to have dinner downstairs in the hotel restaurant, then return to our room for the convocation of spirits.

The room was quaint but had a table the perfect size for a small group of friends to gather around in the hopes that the spirits we wanted to meet would come to us. We lit a single candle and placed it in the center of the table along with several antique objects from my collection of antiques and art objects, jewelry owned by movie stars and props used in the movies. I actually own a pair of cufflinks once worn by Montgomery Clift, a hand mirror used by Marilyn Monroe in her movie *Gentlemen Prefer Blonds*, a gold plated cigarette case given to Mae West by Clark Gable when they worked together in the movie *She Done Him Wrong*, and a rhinestone shoe clip worn by Rudolph Valentino in one of his silent movies. I decided that these trinkets would be perfect to have during the Communication Circle and might attract the spirits of these deceased actors. We weren't sure who, if any, of these spirits would actually make their ghostly presence known to us, but we all believed that by having pieces of their past as tokens they'd know and understand might help our chances of actually contacting these people. As we began the process, we soon found this theory to be correct.

With me this night were Sharon Cohen of Boston, who often accompanies me on investigations and who appears in several of my books, Connie Porter, a medium from British Columbia who was visiting Los Angeles and agreed to help me investigate while she was in town, and Tony Perkins, another psychic who was interested in this sort of thing and who actually knew Monty Clift (as he called him) when they were both young actors.

We each entered a trance state, which is a very relaxed state of consciousness and I instructed the team to hold hands in typical Séance fashion as we all entered the other dimensions together. We breathed together until we were one and held our eyes closed to block out everything that was normal to us in the current time frame.

I led the team into a guided-imagery meditation asking each of them to focus on the movie stars we wanted to connect with. I suggested that they try to see the stars as they remembered them, and as this process took place, our tape recorder hidden in the closet was recording the sounds of the room.

We all were so taken aback with the knocking sounds on the four walls of the small hotel room because the rapping of knuckles on the walls seemed to be from several different pairs of hands in a variety of highs and lows, almost as if the ghosts themselves were playing in a band. There were loud and fast-knocking sounds on the doors of the bathroom and closet as if someone was inside of each of these rooms asking permission to join us in the circle. And there were softer more feminine wrappings at the windows. The table started to jerk violently, popping up and down, and we each opened our eyes to see that the flame of the candle was rising over twelve inches in height above its wick.

I looked at the group and instructed each to ask a question out loud so as to calm the room of spirits down and get them to focus on our questions rather than continue with their unearthly bantering.

The room was filled with presence. Sharon looked at me and suddenly began to channel a male voice who told us he didn't know why he was at the hotel, that the last thing he remembered was sitting outside near his pool in the hills soaking up the sun. We asked the spirit who he was and all he mustered was "Rudy." He then proceeded to ask us if we could make contact with his dearly departed mother *Marie*. As Sharon allowed this spirit to continue to speak with us, the rest of us looked at each other wondering if this was indeed Rudy Valentino. None of us knew enough about the deceased Latin heart throb to know if Marie was indeed his mother's name, but we did know that in his life, Rudy was fascinated with the spirit world, holding his own séances at his various homes throughout Hollywood. He asked us more questions about our time period than we got to ask of his, then the energy diminished until Sharon was thoroughly exhausted and the flame of his spirit left us.

We also heard from several other Hollywood starlets, including Thelma Todd, who swore over and over again that her death was not suicide, but murder. Then she continued to ask for someone named Pat. We later found out that Thelma Todd's former husband was a man named Pat DiCicco who was extremely jealous of Thelma's elite group of friends from the movie industry and wanted her all to himself. Could he have been the murderer?

After several hours of asking questions, we all decided to take a break and went back downstairs and across the street to have some coffee and desert. We'd left the tape recorder on in the closet to see if perhaps we'd receive any EVPs while we were out of the active room. When we returned to the hotel room there was a message for me on the phone's message machine. When I retrieved it, someone from the room next door had called down to the front desk asking if they'd call our room and tell us to stop blowing the horn, that it was bothering her and she couldn't sleep. We looked at each other stunned because we knew none of us were doing such a thing and there was no way anyone could have gotten into our room unless they had a key—I was the only one with the key and we were all together for the hour we left the room.

Tony suggested we check the tape recorder to see if we captured any of the sounds we'd encountered on tape. When we opened the closet door, we found that the two-hour tape had stopped. We rewound the tape and played it to find not only our voices asking questions of the spirits who visited us that night, but in the background the sound of some far away horn being played by someone who didn't know how to play it properly.

Then as we all listened, the sound became louder and we could even make out the tune. It was *When the Saints Go Marching In* and *Amazing Grace*. We also heard the soft manly voice speaking and what sounded like pages being turned roughly then more words. Was this disembodied actor reciting lines for one of his movie roles? We looked at each other and started laughing because we knew it had to be the spirit of Montgomery Clift who came through after we'd left his room. Perhaps the hard knocking we heard on the walls of his former room was a sign that he was trying to scare us, or simply communicate with us that night. His ghost has been reported to be seen in and around that room on the ninth floor near the fire escape.

In many experiences of his ghost, he is holding onto or trying to play a trumpet. It's too bad he didn't come through for us while we sat around that table during our Communication Circle, but we were glad he made contact at all. It was certainly a night none of us would ever forget.

 Jim Morrison

While I've been investigating other haunted sites all over the country, another paranormal experience that I will never forget took place in West Hollywood in the top floor apartment of one of the most famous musicians in Hollywood history: Jim Morrison of *The Doors*. I was hired to conduct an investigation and lead a séance for the TV show *Dead Famous*. The hosts of the show Gail Porter and Chris Fleming accompanied me and the owner of the building. The tenants who resided there and we gathered around a tiny little table to try and make contact with Jim Morrison's ghost who was said to haunt the entire building, but most especially this apartment, the last place he lived in American before heading over to France where he spent the last months of his life.

Maria, the director of the shoot asked me to lead the séance since they knew this was my specialty and that I'd had incredible results with the other segments I was a part of previously on the series. We set up the table that was literally no bigger than three-feet across. It seemed more like an occasional table than a dining room table, but it would have to do. I was filmed walking through the apartment feeling the vibrations to decide where the Communication Circle should be held. The bathroom and dining room both showed unexplainable activity. The cameras showed me unwrapping brand new cassette tapes that we'd inserted into the tape recorders placed in the other rooms to try and record EVP activity. Then we progressed to the area where chairs were set up around the tiny table.

Once I was able to quiet the group including the director, producers, camera people and guests, I asked that everyone hold hands and I led them in a prayer of protection. I felt that this apartment had some evil energy in it and I wanted to make sure that everyone was protected with the white light of the Christ Consciousness, something I always do when I feel negative energy in a place. I must feel completely protected, otherwise I won't stay there.

After the negative energies subsided a bit, I entered a deeper trance state and asked my spirit guides where each participant should sit. This is a very important part of any session so that the energies are balanced. Many times during a session, I'll have people move around to get a better sense of balance before we can continue. Séances can take many hours before anything happens, but this is a wonderful way for people to see spirits in action.

Once everyone was seated, I taught each of the table partners how to breathe taking them into a guided imagery meditative state. I sensed that several of the guests were afraid of what might happen, and even though I asked them to tell me if they were uncomfortable, I knew that two of them were afraid to be embarrassed by agreeing they were scared. I decided to put them at ease by way of a meditation of protection.

The table was so small I had to sit sideways and it was most uncomfortable as I lead the session. I stand six-foot-three inches tall and it was nearly impossible for any of us to keep our knees under the table. I placed a candle in the center. The room was so tight it was nearly impossible for the three camera people to stand around us without actually being seen in the shots themselves. But we did our best.

It suddenly became quite warm as the first few questions escaped the lips of the members present and we started receiving messages from the spirit present who we learned was a young woman who lived in the apartment and died there back in the 1920s when the apartment house was built. We also noticed the chandelier above our heads was moving back and forth very slowly but enough that the cameras were able to pick it up. We all looked upward and watched as the shadows from the arms of the chandelier reflected against the ceiling and darted against it from the glow of the candle—and they truly looked like shadow spirits. I'd placed a bowl of water on the table so the group could actually see the vibrations as the table became a tool of communication itself when the spirits decided to join us.

The table shook and shuddered violently and we all knew that the presence had changed from a woman to a man with this new movement. I asked if this was Jim and the candle flame shot upwards of twelve inches off of the wick before it split in two with air space showing in between the flame in a split second. The camera crew was in awe of the steady presence and the way the table was shuddering as this new masculine spirit made his way around the room answering each of the questions one by one.

One woman asked if he knew where he was and the spirit told me he was in France. A medium acts as the interpreter during a séance and many times the spirits will speak to me telepathically and I then explain their conversations to the group. Another person asked if he was murdered or died of natural causes and nothing happened. In fact, it was as though all of the activity had vanished.

I reminded the person of my rule at the beginning never to ask a spirit how, when, or why they died, because sometimes they don't even know they are deceased and this can cause harm to us and/or the homeowner.

I suddenly felt as though a large animal were under the table and wagging its tail against my legs and thought it was probably some spasm in my legs since I was sitting sidesaddle on the chair. We continued asking our questions and waited for the answers. We'd been at it for over an hour with not much action, other than the candle flame rising up and down in answer to our questions. Then all of a sudden, I felt the same oddity again only this time it felt as though the entity was between the man sitting on my right (one of the tenants who lived in the apartment) and me. I could sense that it was a dog and asked Jim if he had a dog when he lived in this place.

With that question we paused and everyone nearly jumped out of their chairs when we suddenly heard what sounded like a dog howling. Everyone heard it, including the producers, the camera people, and all of the guests sitting around the table. We ended the session shortly after this and were so pleased later when we played back the tapes and heard the dog howling, and found that the cameras had picked it up as well. This was the first time a television program showed actual spirit phenomena on camera.

Victoria Gross Speaks Out: Communicating with Spirits and The Making of a Séance

"The boundaries between life and death are at best shadowy and vague. Who shall say where one ends and where the other begins?"

—Edgar Allen Poe

Victoria Gross surrounded by orbs.

With the advent of paranormal TV shows such as *Medium* and *Ghost Hunters*, talking with the dead has become a more sought after and acceptable pursuit. The internet highway offers unlimited accessibility to anyone wishing guidance on the subject although as with all things, discretion is warranted.

Developing one's mediumship ability is a long and sometimes tedious process. In today's society of instant gratification, there are too many four-week classes with the promise of making one an instant medium. What is not discussed are the pitfalls that one can encounter in the landscape of psychism. As with any ventures into uncharted territory, a roadmap is helpful in making it easier for one to navigate their way through the psychic domain and offered here are some practical suggestions to assist on this road of communicating with spirits. These tips are to be considered only a starting point and not a substitute for proper extended training.

Not everything we read on the internet or in books on the subject should be taken as gospel. I find that the most reliable source of information comes from the Spiritualist Churches, as they have tried and true methods for conducting a séance. Some of my favorite works of knowledge have come from places like The Morris Pratt Institute in Wisconsin, Lily Dale Spiritualist Camp in New York, the book, *So You Want to Be a Medium* by Rose Vanden Eynden, and the works by Echo Bodine. Any of these can safely guide you in the right direction, and all of the above references can be found on the internet.

There are various methods of spirit communication but the séance, having been practiced for centuries, has remained the most popular form of speaking with the dead. Séance is a French word meaning 'seat,' 'session,' and 'to sit.'

The ideal situation for a séance is to have a group of people that one can work with on a regular basis. As with all paranormal investigations, when we work with the same people over a period of time our energies start to mesh and that makes it easier for us as a group to make contact with the deceased.

There are many reasons one may want to contact the spirit world. For some, it is just to establish proof there is life after death while for others no proof is needed and their only wish is to find solace, comfort, and closure. The important thing is that we go into the communication with purpose and respect; respect for the spirit and ourselves and with the understanding that just because someone is dead, that doesn't mean they are smart.

How a person lived their life during their earthly incarnation may carry over into the spirit realm as well, so it stands to reason that a kind, thoughtful person will remain so and a mean and spiteful human being will probably be an unpleasant spirit. We must be in control of the communication at all times.

There is no reason for violent, nasty spirits to visit us during a séance. We wouldn't let some stranger into our homes at might to harm us. We take precautions by locking our doors and we use discretion in picking our friends. The same principles apply when working in the spirit world. We do not leave it up to a spirit to tell us our future or what to do. We must interact with a spirit the same way we do with people on this physical realm. We welcome those who want to befriend us and stay away from those who want to harm us.

To keep negative spirits away, call upon the Guardians of the Gate and ask them to only allow those spirits that you are wishing to make contact with to come through. This prevents unwanted guests and is extremely important. These Guardians, also known as "watchers" and "doorkeepers," are evolved spiritual beings who will then act in the capacity of protectors.

So how do those on the other side know when we are open to communication? As we gather together to prepare for the séance, a beacon of light goes off into the unknown letting those on the other side know that a conversation with the living is now possible, and just as we have our own particular reasons for wanting to contact spirit, they also have their own desires in wanting to communicate with us—be it a loved one who would like us to know they are okay, a murder victim who insists their body and or killer be found, or simply an unknown ghost residing at a haunted location that just wishes to be recognized and heard.

Doing a séance or using a Ouija board can be a challenge for the most learned, let alone the novice. Problems are compounded when someone attempts to achieve something they have little or no knowledge of. The results are minimal, if any, and can sometimes be frightening.

Recently, I took part in a séance that consisted of both seasoned mediums and novices. As the minutes ticked on, the whole atmosphere became more and more chaotic due to lack of focus by some of the participants. All of a sudden, I felt a pressure around my torso. It was as though someone was holding my arms. When I looked down, I saw that my arms were tightly wrapped around my chest in a binding position.

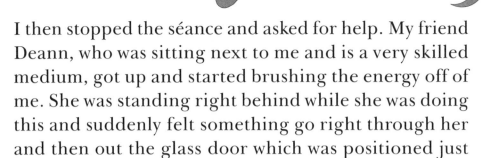

I then stopped the séance and asked for help. My friend Deann, who was sitting next to me and is a very skilled medium, got up and started brushing the energy off of me. She was standing right behind while she was doing this and suddenly felt something go right through her and then out the glass door which was positioned just slightly to her left.

The presence we felt was that of a male energy and he was obviously very controlling. Even though we did a prayer of protection and called in the Gatekeepers to keep watch, the truth of the matter is we negated that request by having so much scattered energy among the participants and allowing people to walk into the séance once it started.

I look at every séance I participate in as a learning session and draw wisdom from the mistakes that are made.

There is quite a big difference between the old-fashion séance of the nineteenth century and what is today called a Communication Circle. First and foremost is the change in the name. Today very few people use the word séance. It has a stigma attached to it and many people still associate séances with fraudulent psychics which were prevalent at the turn of the twentieth century. Another change we find is that in the past, mediums would go into a deep trance and allow the spirit to enter their bodies in order for communication to take place. Today, mediums go into a light mental trance, while all the time being in charge of their faculties and maintaining awareness of their connection with spirit.

Before I go into how to conduct a séance, there are a few things that are important to consider. The first point is an obvious one. When facing a problem in life, you must first search for answers in the living realm. After lots of soul searching and finding no apparent solution, then visit the psychic realm. There has to be a specific purpose for making contact, but remember: Ghosts are not playthings or little puppies that we command at a whim.

Another important thing that cannot be stressed enough is that we must stay in control of the situation, not allow that control to go to the ghost. Validation is also an important process of séances. It is critical that we receive verifiable information from spirit because it is not unusual for a spirit to come through trying to pretend to be someone they are not.

Also, please keep in mind the fact that sometimes spirits cannot always make contact with us. If a person was non- communicative when they were alive, what makes you think they can communicate with us once they are in the spirit realm? Going into a séance with no expectations, an open mind, and the ability to expect the unexpected is helpful since no two séances reap the same results and there are no guarantees that there will be spirit communication.

If one was to do research into séances, they would come upon a myriad of ways to go about it. What is important is that people in the group are all comfortable with the procedure that is chosen and those who are chosen to participate, go into it with the right attitude. Inviting those with negative attitudes, disbelievers, or those not willing to take this type of communication seriously will very likely result in no communication.

Setting the Stage: Location, Time, and Props

Where and when a séance is held really depends on physical availability and time allotted. When investigating a haunted location, it is ideal to hold a séance in that location as the energies of the ghostly visitors can paint us a portrait of who they were and why they are haunting that particular location. If you are just having an ancestral séance, any private location will suffice.

There are two camps of thought and much controversy about when to hold a séance. Many believe that a séance held at night delivers better results, while others do not seem to find much difference between a séance held at night to one held in the day. The argument is that spirits show themselves better at night. But do they, or is it just that the psychic atmosphere is quieter and it is easier to perceive spirits? There have been many séances held in the day that have yielded the same results as séances in the night. It is a matter of personal preference and really doesn't make much difference to a spirit.

It is desirable to choose a quiet location where one will not be disturbed. Not every situation offers the stereotype ambience for performing a séance, so work with what you have.

Another myth that surrounds the subject of communication circles is not to have more than one medium presiding. There have been many times when multiple mediums have sat together adding to the desired outcome. Not every séance will hand over success easily. It takes time and experience and even that is not a sure- fire guarantee.

Many people like to use candles, incense, and music to set the atmosphere. These are wonderful tools to use but are really for the sitter's comfort, to get them in a sedative mood. Spirits generally have no concern about pomp and ceremony. When doing a séance, it is delightful to have all the props and hoopla that goes with the traditional way of thinking in what a séance should look like, though don't miss out on an opportunity to speak with spirit just because there are no props available or it may be in the middle of the afternoon.

The séance is not a dog and pony show and should not be treated like one. Those going into a séance with a demanding and or playing attitude are in for a rude awakening. Too many unwanted things can happen—or nothing can happen. One never knows. Every séance is different and stands on its own merits with the outpouring of changeable results.

The important thing is to be comfortable and know what you are doing. Read as much about the subject that you can get your hands on, go to as many séances as possible, learn all about the pitfalls and how to protect yourself from uninvited guests (both here and there), and most of all, believe in what you are doing. A séance ought to be approached with a sense of reverence, the same as a Sunday service or a ritual. Communication with either the living in this corporeal state or spirits of the beyond is a sacred act.

Step One:
Pick a location where you will be undisturbed for at least an hour. Timing as to when the séance is to preformed is up to the individuals. It is best that a time limit of an hour or two at the maximum be agreed on by the participants, as anything longer than that can be draining on the sitters

and yield futile results. Determine the purpose of the séance. If you can sage the area with a smudge stick to clear away any previous energy, do so. If not, just picture a bright light covering the area and cleansing both your astral field and the geographical astral field that you are in.

Step Two:

Choose an experienced medium and point person. If working with multiple mediums, choose one who will act as the main contact person. A point person ideally ought to be someone who is not the medium. A point person is someone who keeps track of the time and deals with any unforeseen interruptions.

Step Three:

Set up a tape recorder and camera. Once the séance has begun, you don't want to stop to get something you forgot. If candles and incense are desired, this is the time to light them.

Step Four:

The medium sets the tone of the séance by having everyone take a couple of deep cleansing breaths to relax. Release any tension from the mind and body as this helps one to be more receptive to psychic energy. Then state your intention and prayers. These may vary according to one's own belief system. Then call upon the Guardians of the Gate. Look upon them as the hosts of a party. As I mentioned before, when you are preparing for a séance, it's as though a neon light goes off on the other side and advertises a communication party is happening. You are issuing invitation and the Guardians will only allow those spirits to come through that you have put on your guest list.

Step Five:

After the séance is over, thank the spirits who came through for their time and their messages. Also thank the Guardians and anyone else who assisted with protection and their watchful assistance. Let yourself slowly come out of your meditative state and regroup your energy.

Summary:

Physical conditions, receptivity of the group, and communication skills with the spirits are factors that determine if the séance has been a success. It may take more than one séance to establish a conversation with the spirit or it could happen instantaneously. One never knows, as there are no guarantees that the spirit will or can answer. Don't be discouraged if contact is not made on the first attempt. You can always try again at another time.

It cannot be stressed enough that we sitters must remain in control of the situation at all times. A séance is not a parlor game and it is unwise to think of it as such. Knowing what one is doing and what can or cannot happen can never be stressed enough, as more often than not, the unexpected is to be expected.

During the séance or on any other paranormal investigation, pay attention to the little nuances such as smells, extreme temperature change, chills, hearing whispers or voices, and seeing things out of the corner of the eyes. Peripheral vision plays a key role in motion detection and low-light sensation. It has been preserved in the human evolution as part of our survival mechanism. Compound this with the fact that spirit moves at a faster rate in the other worldly dimensions and we begin to understand why we see those images out of the corner of our eyes go by so quickly. They literally move in split second time. That accounts for why most of us second guess ourselves when we do see something. It happens too fast. Our rational mind does not have time to compute the information.

People often ask me how to develop their psychic abilities, and my response is that it is a process that is not done overnight, though the first thing to do and, especially on a ghost tour, is to bring all your attention into yourself. Take a couple of deep breaths and become aware of your body and stay in the present moment. Our skin is the biggest sense organ we have and bringing our attention to the body and the now offers us the opportunity to observe what we otherwise might miss.

I am not totally convinced that one has to be sensitive to psychic energies to have ghostly encounters. I have seen and heard of the most skeptical people and non-believers in the spirit world experience phantom manifestations. From my experience, it appears that ghosts show up when they want and to whom they want. One never knows. My suggestion is go in with an open attitude with no expectations while at the same time being prepared for anything.

Odds, Ends, and Orbs:
A Photo Gallery

"Where'er we tread 'tis haunted, holy ground."

—Lord Byron

Barry Conrad and Victoria Gross **in front of the haunted bank vault** at the corner of Hollywood and Highland.

Looking out at orbs from inside the haunted bank vault.

Hollywood bank basement orbs.

One of the bank basement's long corridors.

More basement orbs in the bank building.

Setting up for the séance in the bank vault.

Scott, Victoria, the author, and Brian setting up for the séance at Scott Michael's house.

Scott Michaels, Scott Woosley, Victoria, and Brian

Victoria and Scott checking out the haunted closet.

Scott's bricks from the Manson murder fireplace.

Queen Mary Hallway orb.

Queen Mary Swimming Pool orbs.

Queen Mary Orbs below deck.

Another Queen Mary Orb.

Contributors

David Wells

David Wells says he had a very ordinary family upbringing in a small Scottish village. His mother worked in a knitwear factory and his father was a coal miner. At the age of sixteen, he joined The Royal Navy, left when he was twenty-four, and began a career in catering within hotels and leisure clubs. In 1991, David decided to go back to college to study leisure as a career, and to fund this he was working forty hours a week as a chef and a waiter in a small hotel in the south of England.

While on Christmas Holiday in Scotland in 1992, David wound up in the hospital, severely ill with pneumonia. As he tells it, "On the second night in hospital I found myself in the corridor being told to go back to bed by an old lady. She said that this is not my time and I have work to do. I did as she asked only to find I was already there! Thinking nothing more than I had been dreaming, I forgot the incident and was released a few days later when improvements to my health were great enough.

I returned to England and was convalescing when I started to experience odd happenings in my home—so odd that I found it impossible to sleep and was looking not so fresh. A friend suggested that I visit a woman who 'knew about these things' and I duly did."

He then went on to learn astrology to ground his abilities, which were showing themselves at an alarming rate. His memory of talking to relatives that had passed over when he was a child came back and he realized that being a psychic medium was his true vocation.

David has most recently been seen on the television show *Most Haunted* on The Travel Channel here in the U.S. and on LivingTV in the U.K. He is the author of *David Wells' Complete Guide To Developing Your Psychic Skills* and *Past, Present and Future: What Your Past Lives Tell You About Your Self* which will be followed by another book on Past Lives coming out late this year.

Visit www.davidwells.co.uk.

Kenny Kingston

Legendary celebrity psychic Kenny Kingston was born to the seventh daughter of a seventh daughter—a very psychic sign.

He credits three women in his life with helping him to develop his psychic ability: his grandmother, Catherine Walsh Clark, taught him to read tea leaves when he was four years old; his beloved mother, Kaye, taught him psychometry (touching an object and picking up psychic vibrations from it) when he was seven; and legendary film immortal (and family friend) Mae West taught him clairaudio (listening to a voice and picking up psychic vibrations) when he was nine years old.

Throughout his childhood and as a young adult, Kenny gave psychic messages and readings to friends and neighbors, many of whom were involved in politics and show business. Word spread and soon he was performing on radio and television, as well as appearing live in lectures.

Kenny has appeared on more television shows than any other psychic, guesting repeatedly on major talk shows around the world. He has hosted his own television series twice—*Kenny Kingston: A Psychic Experience* in the late 1970s in the Los Angeles area; and the syndicated *Kenny Kingston Show* on the East coast during the 1990s.

Kenny has given readings and messages to Marilyn Monroe (he was her one and only psychic), Lucille Ball, Greta Garbo, U.S. Presidents Eisenhower and Truman, Whoopi Goldberg, Phyllis Diller, Howie Mandel, Cindy Williams, and many others. His ties to British royalty began with the Duke and Duchess of Windsor and continued to other members of the monarchy. He has written five books on the psychic world, including his best selling book, *I Still Talk To.*

Kenny lives by the motto: "Only Believe, All Things are Possible if You Only Believe."

Visit http://www.kennykingston.org.

Hans Holzer

Having earned his PhD from the London College of Applied Science, Dr. Holzer has spent over four decades traveling the world to obtain first hand accounts of paranormal experiences, interviewing expert researchers, and developing para-psychological protocols. Over the years, the Viennese parapsychologist has investigated some of the most prominent haunted locations around the world, and he's come as close as a living person can to touching the "other side of life."Hans' latest book is entitled *The Spirit Connection*.

Alexandra Holzer Gargiulo

eing the daughter of the "original" Ghost Hunter, Hans Holzer and Catherine Holzer, a clairvoyant who likes to paint the spirits she meets, it stands to reason that Alexandra, a happily married mother of four is quite aware of life on the Other Side. Soon after her aunt RoseMarie passed on four years ago, she started hearing her voice. "She told me I had to write," says Gargiulo, "and the conversation went from there." And write she did. Alexandra is the author of around twenty children's books, fifty poems, three novels and one novella. Her first in a trilogy of science fiction/ fantasy books called *Lady Ambrosia: Secret Past Revealed* was published in July 2007, followed by an autobiographical tome, *Growing Up Haunted*.

Visit www.hauntingholzer.com.

Victoria Gross

Paranormal researcher and investigator Victoria Gross has been doing professional psychic readings since 1987. Her background is in Tarot, Palmistry, Crystal Gazing, and Psychometry. She also teaches, lectures, and does workshops on these and various subjects relating to metaphysics. Victoria trained at The Arthur Findlay College in England for mediumship, is the founder of The North Orange County Tarot Society located in Southern California, and a member of The International Paranormal Research Organization.

Visit www.noctarot.com.

Barry Conrad

Barry Conrad originally hails from Hamilton, Ohio. When Conrad was twelve years old, he overheard a friend of his mother's discussing the paranormal incidents taking place in her new home on the outskirts of Fairfield, Ohio. Doors would slam shut of their own accord, objects moved around, and the all-pervasive odor of smoke would sometimes filter through the house. One night, her son nearly jumped from the balcony of an upstairs bedroom, feeling that he was being asphyxiated by an invisible fire. Barry was impressed by the woman's apparent sincerity and that lead to his interest in supernatural matters.

He worked as a TV news cameraman at WKRC-TV in Cincinnati working under the auspices of anchorman/reporter Nick Clooney (father of actor George Clooney) and in 1986, Barry moved to California to start his own production company called American Video Features (now known as Barcon Video).

During the fall of 1987, Conrad met Dr. Barry Taff who had once investigated a woman's claims that she had been raped and attacked by an invisible force. The story became a motion picture in 1983 called "The Entity." Thereafter, Taff and Conrad developed a working relationship that lasts to this day, as they have investigated dozens of haunted house and poltergeist cases in the Los Angeles area. In 1989, one of those cases turned out to be nearly as frightening as "The Entity." While checking into a woman's story in San Pedro of malevolent ghostly activity, including the sighting of a disembodied head, the pair encountered violent phenomena. Conrad filmed the case and later made it into a documentary titled "An Unknown Encounter." Segments of the story later appeared in an anthology film that he produced in 2002 called "California's Most Haunted." Both shows garnered high ratings when they aired on the Sci-Fi Channel's *Tuesday De-classified* series in 2003.

Visit www.worldoftheunknown.com.

Michael J. Kouri

Michael J. Kouri has known of his psychic abilities since childhood and is currently the published author of twenty-six books related to the subjects of parapsychology, Psychic Phenomena, and Antiques as he is also an Antique Appraiser who conducts Estate Sales throughout the state of California—many of which have been haunted. He is the creator/producer and host of his own television show: *Investigating the Unknown with Michael J. Kouri* and has appeared on dozens of international television shows with *Barbara Walters* on *The View, 20/20, TV Guide Channel's Pre–Emmy Show with Joan Rivers, KOCE's Real Orange with Rick Milkie,* Warner Bros. production of: *Ghost Ships—Queen Mary* in Long Beach, Ca., French Televisions: *Ghost Hunters of the World,* BBC's *Dead Famous on A&E* and the Discovery Channel, The History Channel's: *Haunted Alcatraz,* The Travel Channel's: *America's Most Haunted Places, & True Hauntings & Ghost Stories of Southern California,* ABC Televisions: *America's Scariest Ghosts Caught on Videotape, Unsolved Mysteries, Mystic Journey's–Haunted Hollywood,* FOX Family Channel's: *Exploring the Unknown,* to name a few...

Visit www.icghosts.com.

Richard Senate

ichard L. Senate was born in Los Angeles, California. His father worked at MGM Studios. Richard attended Long Beach State University earning a degree in history. He says that he saw a ghost, on the night of July 2, 1978, while he was part of an archaeological team at the old Mission San Antonio de Padua in California. It shook him up so much that be began to study ghosts and is now recognized as an expert on the subject. He is the author of fifteen books on the subject of ghosts and local history. His newest book is, *The Illustrated Guide to Haunted Ventura County,* he has appeared on *Sightings, Haunted History* and the *Search for Haunted Hollywood,* as well as *Dead Famous.* He has three children and lives in Oak View, California, with his wife, Debbie Christenson, who he met while doing ghost research. He has visited over 230 haunted houses all over the USA and UK and recently investigated ghosts in Baja Mexico.

Robert James Wlodarski

orn in Los Angeles, California, Wlodarski has BA in history, anthropology, and an MA in anthropology from California State University, Northridge. As the President of Historical, Environmental, Archaeological, Research, Team (H.E.A.R.T.) and Cellular, Archaeological, Resource, Evaluations (C.A.R.E.) since 1978, Wlodarski has administered over 1,400 archaeological and historical projects for federal, state, county, city agencies, and private companies, and has authored and co-authored over twenty articles for journals and magazines throughout California and the Southwest.

Mr. Wlodarski has served as a consultant for: *Catalina, A Treasure from The Past,* for Ironwood Productions; the History Channel/Greystone Productions on their *Haunted History* series; and Consulting Producer with the Food Network on *Haunted Restaurants*; The Travel Channel/ Indigo Productions on their *Most Haunted America* series; Authentic Entertainment/TLC on their *Haunted Hotels* series; Mike Mathis Productions/The Travel Channel on the *Mysterious Journeys* program; and USA TV Special: *Weekend before the Movie—The Whaley House.*

Robert and his wife Anne, founded G-Host Publishing, and have authored and published dozens of books including, *A Guide to The Haunted Queen Mary: Ghostly*

Apparitions, Haunted Catalina: A History of the Island and Guide to Paranormal Activity; The Haunted Alamo: A History of the Mission and Guide to Paranormal Activity; Haunted Alcatraz: A Guide to Haunted Restaurants, Inns, and Taverns; Dinner and Spirits: A Guide to America's Most Haunted Restaurants, Taverns, and Inns; California Hauntspitality: and *Spirits Live: Talking with the Dead.*

Goodbye...

Bibliography

Books:

Holzer, Hans. *The Ghost Hunter's Favorite Cases*. New York: Dorset Press, 2003.

Holzer, Hans. *Elvis Speaks from Beyond and Other Celebrity Ghost Stories*, New York: Gramercy Books, 1993.

Kingston, Kenny, *I Still Talk To...* Santa Ana: Seven Locks Press, 2000.

Web Sites:

http://en.wikipedia.org/wiki/Frank_DeSimone

http://en.wikipedia.org/wiki/Freemasonry

http://en.wikipedia.org/wiki/Hearst_Castle

http://en.wikipedia.org/wiki/Jos%C3%A9_Ferrer

http://en.wikipedia.org/wiki/Rosemary_Clooney

http://en.wikipedia.org/wiki/Russ_Columbo

http://en.wikipedia.org/wiki/S%C3%A9ance

http://en.wikipedia.org/wiki/Spiritualism

http://en.wikipedia.org/wiki/William_Randolph_Hearst

http://mikelehn.com/hollywoodhighland.html

http://pro.imdb.com/name/nm0916067/trivia

http://uk.imdb.com/title/tt0103129/usercomments?start=30

http://www.aboutfamouspeople.com/article1231.html

http://www.amazon.com/Madam-Valentino-Lives-Natacha-Rambova/dp/1558591362

http://www.brainyquote.com/quotes/authors/c/cary_grant.html

http://www.ghostvillage.com/legends/2005/legends35_02072005.shtml

http://www.goldensilents.com/stars/rudolphvalentino.html

http://www.goodfight.org/hwggarbo.html

http://www.hollywoodheritage.org/newsarchive/summer_04/District.html

http://www.keyway.ca/htm2002/whatapos.htm

http://www.laokay.com/halac/RanchoLaBrea.htm

http://www.lapl.org/branches/hist/12-h.html

http://www.latimemachines.com/new_page_8.htm

http://www.lostsouls.tv/extended_pilot.html

http://www.prairieghosts.com/winchester.html

http://www.rosemaryclooney.com/biography.html

http://www.travellady.com/ARTICLES/article-exploringhouse.html

http://www.trivia-library.com/a/history-of-spiritualism-and-seances-part-1.htm

http://www.uncommonjourneys.com/pages/qmlaunch.htm

http://www.winchestermysteryhouse.com/story.html

http://www.allstays.com/Haunted/ca_longbeach_queenmary.htm